SO SAY WE ALL

SO SAY WE ALL

RELIGION, SPIRITUALITY, AND THE DIVINE IN BATTLESTAR GALACTICA

ERICA MONGÉ-GREER

 CASCADE *Books* • Eugene, Oregon

SO SAY WE ALL
Religion, Spirituality, and the Divine in *Battlestar Galactica*

Cascade Books
An Imprint of Wipf and Stock Publishers
199 W. 8th Ave., Suite 3
Eugene, OR 97401

www.wipfandstock.com

PAPERBACK ISBN: 978-1-7252-7336-8
HARDCOVER ISBN: 978-1-7252-7337-5
EBOOK ISBN: 978-1-7252-7338-2

Cataloging-in-Publication data:

Names: Mongé-Greer, Erica, author.

Title: So say we all : religion, spirituality, and the divine in *Battlestar Galactica* / by Erica Mongé-Greer.

Description: Eugene, OR : Cascade Books, 2022 | Includes bibliographical references.

Identifiers: ISBN 978-1-7252-7336-8 (paperback) | ISBN 978-1-7252-7337-5 (hardcover) | ISBN 978-1-7252-7338-2 (ebook)

Subjects: LCSH: Battlestar Galactica (Television program : 2004-2009). | Religion on television. | Television programs—Religious aspects.

Classification: LCC PN1992.77.B354 M66 2022 (print) | PN1992.77.B354 (ebook)

VERSION NUMBER 092922

For all those I give a frak about.
You know who you are.

"We decided to play God, create life. When that life turned against us, we comforted ourselves in the knowledge that it really wasn't our fault, not really. You cannot play God then wash your hands of the things that you've created. Sooner or later, the day comes when you can't hide from the things that you've done anymore."

—ADMIRAL WILLIAM ADAMA, *BATTLESTAR GALACTICA*

CONTENTS

PREFACE | ix

INTRODUCTION | 1

**1 SEASON 1.0
—DEFINING GOD** | 16

**2 SEASON 2.0
—THE WILDERNESS & THE PROMISED LAND** | 36

**3 SEASON 3.0
—COLLABORATION** | 51

**4 SEASON 4.0
—EXISTENTIAL CRISIS & ENLIGHTENMENT** | 67

**5 ETHICAL WARNINGS
AND A CHANCE AT REDEMPTION** | 85

6 CONCLUSION | 100

PREFACE

THE SUBJECT OF RELIGION in science fiction has been growing in my mind as I explored various futuristic fictional universes simultaneously with my seminary education. Years later, while researching for my PhD dissertation, I streamed *Battlestar Galactica* for the third or fourth time through, and with my research notebook beside me, I began jotting down notes about the religious ideas that had drawn me to the show again and again. This was the first seed of the project before you. This book is for science fiction fans who want to explore a little deeper into the social and anthropological connections that tie science fiction and science future to this present world. It's also a book for scholars and religious philosophers who want to think about how popular culture shapes, and is shaped by, the way religion is portrayed.

INTRODUCTION

THE THRILL OF ANTICIPATION for a new science fiction series is like reaching the front of the line for a well-reviewed roller coaster. You know it's going to be great, but the experience of the journey is still just before you. *Battlestar Galactica* is such a ride. It is no wonder that the series appeared as a hyper-comedic exaggeration of binge television in a 2017 *Portlandia* episode sketch entitled "One Moore Episode," where a couple pops in the first DVD of *Battlestar Galactica* on a whim. As they reach for just one more episode, they stop eating, cleaning, or paying the electricity bill, and their lives fall apart for the sake of finishing the series. This sentiment was not an unbelievable exaggeration. I found myself counting down the minutes until I could watch the next episode, even as my partner and I stayed up way past our bedtime to gorge ourselves on the science fiction delight that is *Battlestar Galactica*. That was several years ago, and since then, I have watched the series a handful of times, taking pleasure in getting to know the characters a little more intimately and picking up on the subtle cues that elevate the plot.

A few years ago, I started the series as a downtime activity while writing my dissertation. Wanting a little more out of the experience, I took out my journal and began noting all the little nuances of religious ideology. Religious themes in *BSG* are a subject that came up often for me, and I decided it was time to jot down some of those ideas and thoughts in a more formal way. As I neared the end of the series, I realized there was a rich dialogue in the *BSG* series that centered around religious discrimination, religious ethics, and religious iconography. There were also a number of theological issues and complex conversations about morality that crossed into religious ideas that are held in the real world. *Battlestar Galactica* was a series that took place in an alternate universe. Still, its inhabitants faced discrimination and religious ideology, and faith-versus-science discussions that are familiar in our world today. So, this is a journey to discover what can be learned by exploring religion and theological themes in a science fiction series.

Religion is a very prominent theme in science fiction. Whether dealing with ethical issues between futuristic societies or arguing over the merits of "playing God" with scientific advancements, science fiction has provided a long-standing medium for playing out the social implications of scientific thought. This probably accounts for the fact that people from a wide range of backgrounds, professions, and personal experience are attracted to the genre. And it was no surprise to me when I met a large number of science fiction fans among colleagues at seminary. It turns out that the sort of people who are concerned about the spiritual well-being of people are also worried about how science, technology, and apocalyptic events of the future impact social and personal welfare.

In this book, I start by going over the basic premise and background of the *Battlestar Galactica* series. This is followed by a few remarks on the relationship between religion and science fiction. I then go through each of the four seasons, highlighting ethical and religious themes in the overarching story line. This is followed by a chapter that describes and draws conclusions about particular theological themes that caught my attention. There will be spoilers along the way, and I highly recommend either watching the series before you read this book, or watching each season along the way. If you don't mind knowing the end of a story, feel free to read this book as an introduction to the series. I find that I can still enjoy the story even if I know what's going to happen. So, choose your method and ready-check your transport, because we are heading

to outer space with the last remnant of the human population, and
don't forget to say a prayer—So say we all.

A BRIEF INTRODUCTION
TO BATTLESTAR GALACTICA

Battlestar Galactica (TV series, 2004–9), or *BSG*, was developed
by Ronald D. Moore. Moore reimagined the original *Battlestar
Galactica* (TV series, 1978) for a modern audience, launching this
version in a way that encouraged viewers to wrestle with ethical
questions geared to survivors in a post-9/11 world. The series
quickly gained a cult following, which prompted the release of
supplemental films, *Battlestar Galactica: Razor* (2007), *Battlestar
Galactica: The Plan* (2009), *Battlestar Galactica: Blood & Chrome*
(2012), a TV series prequel, *Caprica* (2009–10), and a yet-to-be-
released new *Battlestar Galactica* film and series.[1] In addition
to professional productions, *BSG* fans carry out conversations
through social media outlets, including Reddit, Facebook, Twitter,
meme-creation sites, and more. An internet search for *Battlestar
Galactica* captures more than twelve million results. What the frak
does all this mean? It means that you should close this book, find
out where *BSG* is currently streaming, and watch it immediately.

BSG has a reputation for being grounded, humanistic, sexy,
and gritty while dealing with important human issues like patriotism, genetic engineering, democracy, religious freedom, and
discrimination. These issues aren't new to science fiction. Still,
Ronald D. Moore presented a futuristic human population that
was not polished, like so many versions of the future. He told a
story of redemption through seriously flawed, humorous, witty,

1. Sam Esmail updated his progress in an interview on January 27, 2021,
stating that the new *Battlestar Galactica* will not be a reboot of the story Ronald D. Moore produced. Furthermore, it will be released on NBC's streaming
service, Peacock, when it is ready. Also announced, director Simon Kinberg
will write and produce a separate *Battlestar Galactica* movie, details to come.
  Gary Collinson, "Sam Esmail Gives an Update on Peacock's *Battlestar Galactica* Reboot." https://www.flickeringmyth.com/2021/01/
sam-esmail-gives-an-update-on-peacocks-battlestar-galactica-reboot/.

self-obsessed, ambitious, and deeply troubled characters. Ultimately, the story is one of hope, reconciliation, and awareness of self, even as the minutiae of humanity are under a microscope for critical evaluation. *BSG* raises a lot of serious questions in entertaining ways, but good doesn't always win out, and even when victory comes, it is often saddled with a frakked-up mess. While some science fiction stories are polished and maybe even safe to leave alone with your pre-teen, *BSG* is one you may want to monitor as some of the issues raised can hit a little too close to home (which we will look out for more in-depth in this book!).

The world of *BSG* is rich with mythical history and religious ideology that extends from the beginnings of human civilization to the origins of the Cylon: humanity's created AI species. Aside from the social references to supernatural concepts like fate and destiny, there are specific religious tribes and accompanying political manifestations. The Cylons, though considered children of humanity, follow their own religious ideals that even vary among themselves, resulting in a variety of religious factions. It is fair to say that religion is as much a theme in *Battlestar Galactica* as anything else (and maybe even more so!). The *BSG* universe has not shied away from developing a technologically advanced world where religion has evolved in multiple ways for both humans and Cylons. Many religious ideals in *BSG* represent current real-world religious beliefs and the implications of such beliefs. Exploring religion in *BSG* is one way we can evaluate our own present reality and find better ways to communicate who we are and why we believe the way we do.

This book explores the series while critically reflecting on ethical questions that have been an important part of religious culture for millennia. Some of these topics include the value of human life, death and grief, divine will, free will, and democracy. Even though the religion in *BSG* is fictional, with fictional roots, its inspiration comes from real-world religious concepts and ideas about religion. One great thing about science fiction stories is they take our problems and launch them into outer space, where we can see the bigger picture a little more clearly, and, more specifically, gain a more objective external perspective. While this project is an ethnographic exploration of a fictional version of the future of humanity, reflecting on *BSG*'s universe may shed some light on our own world, and I think the point is that we stop and take a look at where we've been and where we're headed before we end up making mistakes that have only so far been imagined.

To encourage reflection and further exploratory conversation about religious values in *BSG*, this book takes an anthropological approach, moving from season to season, breaking down major plot points as they relate to understanding the religion of the Capricans, other colonists, and the Cylons. A detailed description of human and Cylon populations will be outlined in the summary of the *BSG Miniseries*, included toward the end of this chapter, and also in the next chapter, which focuses on the first season.

A NOTE ABOUT THE GENRE

Science fiction (sci-fi) developed as a genre for scientists to explore the implications of technological advancement in futuristic simulation. One of the most remarkable side-effects of exploring futuristic science, where technology created a new paradigm for humans, was to hold a mirror to humanity and also invite speculation about behavior, psychology, and religion. This is what makes sci-fi such an excellent medium for exploring humanity's themes, including (and, I would argue, especially) when it comes to religious expression.

Science fiction is a type of speculative fiction. Speculative fiction imagines an alternate reality, human interaction with futuristic technology, or engagement with unknown species. Speculative fiction asks the reader to withhold logic or suspend reality to enjoy a story. Sometimes this suspension of disbelief is small and singular in an otherwise realistic world. For example, a story that allows a person to fly. All other things being equal for the world, many entertaining stories could be told with this exciting imaginable element. Other times, the suspension of disbelief is greater and more complex. For example, imagine a larger, fantastic world, where several species interact and zip around in spaceships between planets and have built technology that far exceeds modern abilities. For the sake of the story, an audience might suspend disbelief to engage in such fantasies. Science fiction tells these kinds of stories and is considered a subgenre of speculative fiction. To understand sci-fi as a genre, it is helpful to understand the nuances of reception. Sci-fi is often categorized as "hard" or "soft," although, it becomes a purely intellectual discussion to classify individual works.

Sci-fi can also be an extensive category. There are many philosophical debates to be had, parsing out fantasy from science fiction. Guidelines have been proposed but hardly established. Each time a new work of fiction is published, it influences the boundaries of sci-fi. I will lay out a general thrust of terms and definitions but will not attempt to assert finality. There is a wide array of science fiction, some of which has been called "hard" science fiction to distinguish it as strictly adhering to scientific principles. Hard science fiction explores the scientific quality of its futuristic world against rigorous known data in the STEM fields. By comparison, "softer" sci-fi makes bigger leaps in technology development, and sometimes it includes fantastical elements. Since categories are not regulated, these terms are not very helpful in a systematic way. However, the language of hard and soft science has been used to explore and categorize themes in the broader genre of speculative fiction. These categories are arbitrary and may be understood in a variety of ways. One idea is that social sciences (sometimes referred to as the "soft" sciences) are at the heart of "soft" science fiction, but this is a misalignment of terms. Matters of social science are intrinsically connected with the hard sciences. Even though social sciences and hard sciences exist as very separate entities, science fiction unites the two fields of study. Science fiction literature mirrors life, in which human social behavior influences, and is influenced by, scientific technological advances. The science fiction genre draws on scientific terms and principles to describe one's universe while at the same time weaving a human story that involves cultural, societal, political, religious, and social values. The genre of science fiction may broadly incorporate qualities of science in a descriptive, rather than prescriptive, way, and I'll leave it for systematicians to parse the lexicon in a more detailed manner.

To test the implications of futuristic technologies, science fiction places technology in the hands of humans and measures the outcome, speculating about how societies and individuals will respond to particular technology and advancements. This is achieved through storytelling. Agents in the narrative actively or passively engage with the creation or implementation of science theory and practice, and the consequential world builds the setting for a futuristic story.

Science fiction in its earliest forms made magical leaps in technology. Mary Shelley's *Frankenstein* (1818) is often identified as the first science fiction novel, in which a synthetic life-form proves its sentience. Her exploration of the events leading up to the creation of Frankenstein's monster includes a combination of actual applied science known in that time, as well as arbitrary leaps in biological function and reaction. In Shelley's novel, Dr. Frankenstein is a scientist who is obsessed with achieving the impossible: bringing the dead to life. Dr. Frankenstein, in his compulsion, builds and then animates an unnamed creature, consequentially discovering Artificial Intelligence (AI). While scientific research and methodology are clearly included in the storytelling, most of the story revolves around the philosophy of humanity and discerning what it means to be alive or sentient. In the subtext, Shelley poses questions about what it means to be human. Can a human lose their humanity? And likewise, can an artificial life-form gain humanity? Does the want of a mate and like-companion demonstrate the existence of a soul? These are some of the questions that Frankenstein's monster explores in his journey of philosophical awareness. These questions have been raised in science fiction ever since.

AI is not merely a theoretical futuristic idea. It is a construct at work in the present world. Social networking incorporates AI as an infrastructure that assists the cooperation between computer-generated algorithms and human users. As a result, AI algorithms anticipate the needs of human users in searching for and accessing information. Most people interact with forms of AI regularly through social media accounts like Facebook, Twitter, and Instagram. Even news is delivered through AI. Sci-fi is inspired by the real-time use of technology and smooths the story by painting in the details. Through sci-fi literature, we get a picture of an AI that is external and substantial in form. *BSG* shows a glimpse of the progression of current developments and robotic technologies that suggest we are heading toward the same trajectory as the Capricans, a decision we might come to regret.

Some other examples of AI in sci-fi include the Positronic lifeform AI, Data, in *Star Trek: The Next Generation* (1987), the Emergency Medical Hologram (EMH) in *Star Trek: Voyager* (1995), and a handful of main characters on *Humans* (2015). An episode of *Doctor Who*, written by Neil Gaiman, portrays the TARDIS as a sentient AI, and many other sci-fi stories and cinematic productions represent future human/AI interactions. These include *Her* (2013), *AI* (2001), *Bicentennial Man* (1999), *Do Androids Dream of Electric Sheep?* (1968), *Blade Runner* (1982), and many others.

British author Arthur C. Clarke laid the groundwork for modern science fiction by describing how science should be conceived and used in the future. While Clarke is esteemed as a more "scientific" (hard) science fiction writer, Clarke's various laws and rules of order apply ethical consideration to scientific advancement, which blends his work into social (soft) science and humanities concerns. Clarke's three rules became sci-fi guidelines for technology, many of which are still regarded in modern sci-fi literature:

"1) When a distinguished but elderly scientist states that something is possible, he is almost certainly right. When he states that something is impossible, he is very probably wrong.

2) The only way of discovering the limits of the possible is to venture a little way past them into the impossible.

3) Any sufficiently advanced technology is indistinguishable from magic."[2]

Isaac Asimov is another prominent name in modern science fiction. Asimov laid the groundwork for what sorts of rules should be put in place for artificially intelligent beings created by humans, more commonly known as "robots." According to the Oxford English Dictionary, Asimov is credited with inventing the term "robotic," from which he formulated the "Three Laws of Robotics":

> First Law—A robot may not injure a human being or, through inaction, allow a human being to come to harm.
> Second Law—A robot must obey the orders given it by human beings except where such orders would conflict with the First Law.
> Third Law—A robot must protect its own existence as long as such protection does not conflict with the First or Second Law.[3]

BSG pushes the limits of "impossible" in human exploration capabilities. In the series, twelve distinct colonies of human populations have colonized an equal number of planets in their galaxy. They have also succeeded in developing artificial, sentient, intelligent life-forms. The series also questions the ethics of Asimov's robotics laws in light of "free will," leading the viewer into philosophical territory that is not unlike the difficulties faced more than two centuries ago by Frankenstein's monster.

The show's creator and director, Ronald Moore, had previously worked as a writer for Gene Roddenberry's *Star Trek: The Next Generation*. Moore prioritized storytelling whenever explaining the science threatened to complicate matters. He once said in an interview, "We *always* tried to make drama work with science on *BSG*, but when push comes to shove, drama wins."[4] However, science remains a big part of sci-fi, and seeing how much sci-fi

2. Arthur C. Clarke, *Profiles of the Future: An Inquiry into the Limits of the Possible* (London: Harper & Row, 1962), 14, 21, 21n1.

3. Isaac Asimov, *I, Robot* (New York: Doubleday, 1950), back cover.

4. Patrick Di Justo and Kevin R. Grazier, *The Science of* Battlestar Galactica, (Hoboken, NJ: Wiley & Sons, 2011), 5 (emphasis original).

authors like their rules of three, fans found it helpful to consider these established Three Laws of the Science of *Battlestar Galactica*:

The First Law takes care of the lack of scientific explanation, the unresolved plot issues, and the fleet's endless supply of whiskey: "If you're wondering how they eat and breathe, and other science facts, just repeat to yourself, 'It's just a show, I should really just relax.'"

The Second Law is a quote from Carl Sagan; "Space is mostly empty. That's why it's called 'space.'"

The Third Law is: "All of this has happened before and will happen again." Don't lose sight of this.[5]

For those fans who want to geek out over the science in *Battlestar Galactica*, you can take a look at *The Science of Battlestar Galactica*, by Patrick Di Justo and Kevin R. Grazier, with a foreword by *BSG* producer Jane Espenson. And this book is for those who want to explore the religion, the mythos, and the philosophical quest for meaning.

NAVIGATING ETHICS AND MORALITY IN SCI-FI

This project primarily deals with the cinematic representation of sci-fi. As previously stated, the genre allows for investigation into the future based on current technological advancements in STEM fields. The primary underlying factor to all this—the creative writing, film production, and consideration for scientific progress—is that all areas impact, and are impacted by, humans. Science without regard for humanities is just data. It calls out for interpretation. Science fiction makes space for human interpretation and decision-making. This is where an evaluation of ethics and moral consideration is most beneficial.

The stories evolving from scientific perspectives in many ways reflect more about who we are as a people and what we expect from humanity than what we can achieve with scientific advancement.

5. Di Justo and Grazier, *Science of* Battlestar Galactica, 6.

The intent might be to focus on the quantifiable aspects of technological advancement, but the result is the illumination of the quality of human existence. As a genre, sci-fi has become a way to explore what it means to be human. This is often achieved by seeing an encounter with humans through the eyes of an AI form. Morality is a central theme in these encounters, whether it is dealing with how and why people go to war, the impact of colonization, interracial or interspecies conflict, or, of course, religion.

Religion is invariably addressed in some form or other in most sci-fi stories. Sometimes religion is an outmoded idea of the past. Sometimes it is militaristic, and sometimes religion is represented by a conflagration of several philosophical ideals. Religion in sci-fi becomes one way of identifying ethical values and moral pitfalls surrounding human engagement with future STEM technologies. Often this is explored by technologies and advancements which influence, or are influenced by, religious ideas. This works both ways. Religious ethics sometimes encourage or discourage how technology is developed, or if its use is permitted.

Religion itself is a prominent theme throughout *BSG*. It is so heavily a part of the story line that the prequel, *Caprica*, develops a complex backstory to explain the religious divergence between the Cylons and the Capricans. While this current work seeks to explore the relationship of Cylons and humans and their respective gods, it also develops a discussion of how people from different religious backgrounds can find their way toward common ground, and if that is even possible. The struggle of self-identity and the resulting struggle of accepting the "other" is a significant theme in the series and offers an opportunity for reflection. By viewing this struggle as an ethical dilemma, we may then explore our own experiences with defining the self, our community(ies), and how we are inclined to discriminate against those different from us.

In *BSG*, religious ideas evolve and also mirror our own various religious beliefs in the present world. With the series, we are allowed to observe as outsiders, to watch an imaginary society with different religious structures discover itself, doubt itself, and reexamine belief systems. We are also then invited to examine our prejudices and to explore our belief systems. The series encourages reflection on the essence of religion. Questions about belief and faith are implicitly raised throughout the story: When do the ends justify the means for religiously motivated actions? Can two different religions make a compromise to live or work together peaceably? Do creation and progeny have religious value? How are religious values prioritized when the world is changing everything about society? Is there a supreme species or race, and how is that determined?

Sci-fi is a genre that encourages the imagination of futuristic scenarios based on current scientific trajectories, but the entire story is so much more. Sci-fi invites every person, by means of another universe, to get to know our prejudices, concerns, fears, and hopes by watching another society of like-minded people explore their world. In this way, sci-fi offers a cautionary tale of ethics and morality for consideration. Without instructing us, as consumers of the story, how to respond, we may choose to engage and explore or turn our backs on the rich portrayal of the complex nature of humanity. When asked about the importance of science in *BSG*, co-producer Jane Espenson responded, "The point of *Battlestar Galactica* was not, ultimately, science. It was a show about the human condition, hope, and moral grayness."[6] The science is essential, and its qualifications are impressive and necessary, but there is so much more to think about. An overarching theme in *BSG* that is both ethical and theological has to do with determining the value of human life. This is done in various episodes on an individual level by looking at repopulation issues by procreation, abortion, inherited labor, and prison colonies. But, it is also considered in broader sweeps in light of human-Cylon relations and identity formation.

---

6. Di Justo and Grazier, *Science of* Battlestar Galactica, xiii.

BSG TELEVISION MINISERIES

One year before *BSG* began its four-season arc, the *BSG Miniseries* was produced as a two-part pilot that may now be seen as a movie-like introduction to the entire series. The miniseries establishes the premise of the series and introduces essential characters. In the miniseries, viewers learn the basic premise of the conflict between Cylons and humans, while characterization and story arcs for the main characters are established.

The opening scene shows a lone human military person seated at a simple desk in the middle of a large room. The spacious and empty surroundings communicates a straightforward fact: he doesn't expect anything to happen here. But, this is the beginning of a story, so this is the day that something happens. Enter the unexpected. A beautiful woman in a bright red, fitted dress enters the station, flanked by two Cylon Centurions. She approaches the man, kisses him, and then kills him. So much for peace talks. The destruction of humanity has now begun.

We then move to Caprica City, the central station of the Twelve Colonies. Caprica City is a point of convergence for all that humanity offers: its diversity, achievements, and self-indulgence. The human capacity for self-pleasure and self-gratification is a central premise, begging the question that the series poses repeatedly: Does humanity deserve to be saved? This particular question is raised after the miniseries in Commander William Adama's speech when he says, "Why are we as a people worth saving?" He proceeds to hint at his dissent, stating, "Sooner or later, the day comes when you cannot hide from the things you've done anymore."[7] Adama presents for consideration the evidence of humanity's hubris regarding the creation, and subsequent discarding, of the Cylons. The stakes are high. Humanity's worth is on trial.

Dr. Gaius Baltar is the first human we meet. He exemplifies the extreme hedonist, portraying a self-indulgent elitist who enjoys the fame and attention of the media, as well as a significant

---

7. *Battlestar Galactica: The Miniseries.* S1, Ep1, directed by Michael Rymer, written by Ronald D. Moore and Glen A. Larson, 0:41:57–0:42:58.

number of beautiful lovers. One of them is the soon-to-be-revealed Caprica Six Cylon, brilliantly portrayed by Tricia Helfer. Dr. Baltar represents the indulgent capital city, Caprica, and while his character serves as a kind of comedic foil throughout the series, his narcissism is recognizable. We can then examine our own culture at the heights of prosperity and indulgence to subsequently fill in the gaps about Caprica and its denizens.

The initial conflict is Us-versus-Them. The Cylons have evolved over the past several decades to become masters over the technology that was initially the invention of humankind. After the Cylons detonate a nuclear warhead in Caprica, killing nearly everyone on the planet and making most of the surface unlivable, the remnant human population must rely on older technology for survival. Enter the show's namesake, *Battlestar Galactica*, an old warship scheduled on that very day to enter retirement as an obsolete military vessel, along with its commander, William Adama, whose career had found an exit aligning with the retirement of the old ship and its accoutrements. After the Cylon attack on Caprica City, both the ship and its commander are recalled to action.

The Cylons are motivated by a strong belief that God has chosen them to replace their human creators as the Elect. Because God has willed it, the Cylons carry out the destruction of humanity by the most efficient means possible. The ends justify the means. Six is arguably the most devout of the Cylon models. She repeatedly attributes God as the one who inspires her to instigate nuclear warfare to eradicate all humans. This is the work of a religious terrorist. The ends justify the means, even when she will sacrifice herself in the process.

Since humans do not respect the Cylons as anything more than machines created to serve humans purposefully, they refer to them as "toasters" and then later as "skin jobs," nicknames that keep them *othered*, as enemies. This complication will come to bear on future human-Cylon interactions throughout the series. The othering of an enemy is a common strategy in the military. It is meant to keep people focused and unsympathetic toward the enemy faction.

The human effort to fight the Cylons is primarily motivated by self-preservation as a species. To keep this motivation, they fight to keep an Us-versus-Them mentality in view. The Cylons are nothing, but the humans are measured by counting "souls." The number of souls is an essential concept in the series. President Roslin holds on to this number, an up-to-date census of humans remaining alive among the fleet, as a sign of human fragility as well as hope for the future. Where there are some, others will follow. What they don't know yet is that Cylons are inadvertently counted as humans, since they are scattered among the fleet.

At first, the discrimination against the enemy on each side is simple and straightforward. The Cylons view humanity as a relic of the past, whose evolution has halted. They seek to destroy them and take their place as the species of the future. The Cylons each describe this sentiment in different ways. At one point, the Cylon Leoben proposes that God may have made a mistake the first time around and has now decided to give souls to the Cylons. Gaius also brings this up in the course of time, reiterating the Cylons' theological position. This recognition foreshadows Gaius's slow path to conversion to faith in the Cylon god. More importantly, Gaius's statement is echoed in Adama's reflection about the value of humanity.

The stakes raised in BSG include measuring the worth of a human population that has lost most of its members in an enemy assault. They do not readily give up the fight for self-preservation, but they have been asked to consider if the Cylons are not justified in their action.

By introducing the series this way, BSG has laid out for consideration the value of humanity and asked the question central to many religions, a theological question which is explored deeply in religious texts: Is any of humanity worthy of salvation?

— 1 —

SEASON 1.0 —
DEFINING GOD

BSG ENGAGES THE VIEWER with quick action that dives deep into the story, unveiling the conflict between humans and Cylons. While it is not necessary to watch the *BSG Miniseries* first, it does help to get an initial idea of the basic premise and the individual story arcs for character development. Still, no punches are pulled in the first episode, "33." The Cylons follow the Colonial Fleet that carries the remnant human population across the galaxy to complete the annihilation of the human race. William Adama commands the sole remaining military vessel, leading a fleet of space vessels that are civilian operated and civilian inhabited. The Cylons, whose evolution has exceeded the wildest imagination of the colonials, seem to have an inside track on the fleet's location. I dare anyone to watch the first episode of *BSG* and walk away. There is a dramatic tension that triggers interest. It is great storytelling at least.

BSG has received praise for an outstanding cast of actors that worked together so well and so inclusively that it made an easy go of portraying a tightly knit community of remnant human characters in the series. Each character is introduced in the first season with their accompanying strengths and weaknesses. Humanity is on the verge of a new world order, and humanity's leaders have loads of baggage weighing upon this newly formed society. There is a constant expectation for life to return to normalcy, mixed with an underlying awareness that things can never be the same again.

We get so many big and existential questions in season one: "What is the value of a soul?" "Who is responsible for maintaining order?" "Why does it seem like some people are more important than others?" These questions, and others, have to do with social order and awareness of independent communities. What does it mean for a survivor of such an attack to identify as a particular nationality when there is only one nation left, the remnant human population?

We also get several explicitly religious questions in season one, such as, "Who or what is a god?"; "Can a being created by a human still gain access to God or an afterlife?"; "Who can have a relationship with the divine?"; "Is there such a thing as prophecy?"; and "What is the role of prayer?" These questions have both explicit and implicit bearing throughout the *BSG* series.

In Caprica, praying and cursing in the name of the "Lords of Kobol" is typical behavior, but it is not done in a devout manner. Religion is experienced casually in Caprica. There are few religious leaders and they seem to inhabit the margins. There is no recognized central religious authority, yet religious expressions permeate the culture. The influence of a past religious culture lingers in the swears and prayers of the humans.

In the series, there is one human priest whose presence is evidence of an historical respect for religious tradition. She becomes a member of President Laura Roslin's advisory team as a symbolic gesture to those marginal colonies who are more religiously inclined. The priest keeps the religious scrolls. They contain prophecy, prayer guides, and apparently, a map to Earth and the thirteenth colony. As the series develops, we learn that the people furthest away from the Caprican heart of the human colonies are more likely to be more familiar with the ancient scripture.

There is also an implicit contrast between religion and science. This will come up in particular ways, especially in "The Woman King," an episode in season three that looks at medical ethics and freedom of religion. But, more generally, it appears in season one through *Galactica's* resident scientist, Dr. Gaius Baltar. Even in the first episode, he advocates for the destruction of a civilian ship because he learns a Cylon is aboard who might compromise his secret. When one of the administrative personnel thanks the lords of Kobol for Gaius, Gaius gives an agnostic response, dismissing the idea that a divine power could have guided him there. Gaius shows us over and over again that science is in stark contrast to religious beliefs. At the same time, Head Six, so named by fans because she exists only in Gaius's head, continues to try and convert him to believe in the Cylon God[1] as the "One True God." She urges him to repent of his sins and accept God's love. Hers is a message of salvation through forgiveness in response to the confession of sins. The message sounds very familiar to real-world Christianity. It is sometimes tricky in *BSG* to separate the fiction from the real world.

FIRST SEASON CHARACTERS

Before we jump into the season summary and major religious issues, it will be helpful to take a brief look at the characters in *BSG*. The defining factions are Cylons and humans. As the series progresses, smaller groups and factions distinguish themselves from the crowd, and the lines between "us" and "them" get blurred. Complexities aside, introductions will follow the format of Cylons, then humans.

MEET THE CYLONS

In the first season, we meet a whole new species, the Cylon. Cylons are AI that evolved from robotic technology created by humans on Caprica. The series does a great job of showing us who the Cylon

---

1. The Cylons believed in one true capital-G God as opposed to the human population who believed in multiple deities without clear hierarchical distinction. The Cylons' God is meant to relate more closely with our world's monotheistic (Abrahamic) faiths.

is by introducing various Cylon characters. Simultaneously, we quickly understand the human perception of the Cylon.

Humans view Cylons as "toasters," a derogatory stereotype that diminishes the species by referring to Cylons as a mechanical tool built by humans with a singular purpose—to serve humanity. The Cylon is the enemy. They rose and waged war against the humans, their creators, and humans have been pretty bitter about it ever since. Regardless, they built an armistice station in neutral space, which was maintained as an attempt at possible diplomacy. Even so, it becomes quickly apparent that most of the human population sees robotics as a failed experiment and believes they would be better off without the Cylons.

The Cylons seek unification in an ordered autocracy. Their government stems from their ability to connect psychologically. They cannot link this way with humans, which may partly explain why they view humans as lower-order beings, weaker, and less capable. The Cylons define themselves as humanity's children, but they also consider themselves an evolutionary progression of humanity, and simultaneously, favored by God above their human creators.

The audience learns ahead of the colonials that the Cylons have taken on human form and are thus indistinguishable from humans. There are several models of each of seven Cylon prototypes and five more Cylon models yet to be revealed. The models are identified by numerical assignment, although as the series progresses, individual Cylons distinguish themselves and gain individual names. Dr. Gaius Baltar is the first character to learn about the new form of the Cylon, but that is only because he is sleeping with a Cylon. Enter Six.

The Six Cylon is the first model we meet. She is very sexualized, and is often portrayed on the cover artwork for the series in her signature bright red dress. She is a central character in the series, and she has been portrayed in a *BSG* version of *The Last Supper*, where she inhabits the space belonging to Christ.

The Six is immediately set up as a foil for the audience. She is alluring and attractive, with expensive taste and impressive gravitas. Six moves in languid strides. She appears to be human but is just shy of normal. She is introduced with one of the most disturbing and fascinating sequences in the beginning of the mini-series. Six approaches a mother with a stroller and asks to look more closely at her baby. She is clearly fascinated and we later find out that she longs to have her own child. When the human mother turns her back for a few seconds, Six wonders at the vulnerability of the baby, and proceeds to snap the baby's neck, quietly and quickly. She has walked away quite a distance before the mom screams in the background after realizing her baby is no longer breathing. The viewer is quickly bent against Six, immediately sympathizing with the humans against their Cylon enemies. We are conditioned to cheer for the weaker, more vulnerable population—the humans are the David to the Cylon Goliaths. At the same time, the Cylon enemies worship the one true God, which is also a point of connection for many viewers who can identify with their ardent belief in one God. Battlestar Galactica messes with our loyalties, leading us to side with one race and then another until the complexities overtake us and we surrender, forgiving everyone their past incarnations. Caprica Six (as this particular model will become known), comforts herself with the thought that she is saving the baby from a more painful death due to the impending nuclear destruction. She is single-minded in her role as a covert terrorist. She has seduced Dr. Gaius Baltar, the lead scientist on a project she needed access to in order to complete her mission. What she didn't plan for was an unexpected human emotion: love. Even though Baltar failed to fully return her affection, she loves him. She shields him from the blast of the explosion, saving his life with the sacrifice of her own body. When she resurrects, this emotional attachment sets her apart from other Cylons, even among her own model. This eventually leads her to share in a unique position of leadership with Boomer, who has experienced something similar in an entirely different way.

Boomer is a pilot on the *Galactica*. She is also a "sleeper" Cylon, a Model Eight. She is smart, funny, and generally well-liked. She is also caught up in a romantic relationship with Deck Chief

Tyrol. Throughout the first season the *Galactica* experiences a series of attacks by sabotage, and Boomer discovers evidence that she is unknowingly involved. She suspects she is a Cylon and because she is so much aligned with the humans, she even tries to destroy herself. She is a tragic character at the beginning of the series. The first season's finale sees Boomer in handcuffs after she shoots Adama in the chest at close range. This event sets into motion an existential crisis for both Boomer and Adama. They each have considered themselves family in service to the *Galactica*. To find out that Boomer was in fact one of the enemy is shocking, and Adama continues to especially wrestle with the philosophical consequences of this revelation. He is particularly bothered by the fact that she felt like a daughter to him. Adama's response to the incident raises the question, and not for the last time: How do we determine who is "us" and who is "other"? In a conversation with Tyrol, Adama asks him if he loved her. Tyrol solemnly replied that the relationship felt like love. What is the difference? Adama responded that it's the same thing: feeling love for someone is indistinguishable from loving them. This is an important theme that emerges in season two, adding complexity and dimension to the relationships between human and Cylon, between creator and creature. Learning that Boomer is a Cylon blurs the lines of "us versus them," and encourages viewers to think about a person's worth. We are also led to think about what right one person has to decide if another lives or dies. Even though in this case it was a Cylon killing a human, when the tables are turned, the humans feel justified in their own violent actions.

We also meet another Model Eight Cylon, who becomes known as Sharon Agathon. She passes for Boomer on Caprica and engages in a romantic relationship with Helo, who remained on the planet in order to allow more people to be shuttled back to the fleet. She and Helo are the first to procreate. Their baby becomes the Cylon-human hybrid that represents the shape of things to come. Eventually, Sharon earns her own place in service aboard the *Galactica*. Even though she is very different than Boomer, her story also blurs the lines of who should live and who should die.

It is a question that is asked over and over again throughout the series.

While seeking weapons at a remote armory, Adama runs into the Cylon Leoben. He is a philosopher and engages Adama in a conversation about the meaning of life and the significance of existence. His model reappears in the fleet at a later time and before flushing him out of an airlock, Starbuck interrogates him by means of torture. It is suggested that the normal laws against torture do not apply when the enemy is a "machine," but the distinction keeps getting muddled. It is clear that Leoben gets through to Kara Thrace on a personal level, something that comes back to haunt her in a later season. He is the philosopher, the "suffering servant" of the Cylons. He is willing to endure rejection, abuse, torture, and even death, in order to see that the prophecy is revealed and respected.

Aaron Doral is a Cylon who inadvertently becomes the scapegoat for sabotage on the *Galactica*. His model appears later as a suicide bomber. Finally, the Cylon Simon is introduced as a doctor on Caprica, running experimental hybridization of Cylon-human babies.

And that's four Cylon models. Three more of the so-called Significant Seven will be revealed in the second season, and the Final Five will be revealed later in the series.

MEET THE HUMANS

The human characters represent another side of the story in every season. In *BSG*, humans have just had their power stripped away by a species of their creation. They are eminently vulnerable, and, at the same time, they bear a burden of responsibility for their present state. Humans are like gods themselves. The gods they worship—Zeus, Athena, Apollo—are also their ancestors, and they have risen to heights of power and expansion throughout the universe. They have created life and then set out to destroy it. Now, the creator is hunted by its creature, and the viewer is called upon to judge between them.

Dr. Gaius Baltar is the first human we meet in the series. He was saved from the explosion by his Cylon Six companion, and he was rescued and delivered aboard *Galactica*. He is a well-known scientist, with particular expertise in advanced technology. Gaius is a man of science and reluctant to engage in any serious conversation about religion. However, his journey is one of conversion. He is influenced by Head Six, his companion.

Commander William Adama is the military leader in the new world order of *BSG*. He is seasoned and experienced in military command, having fought in the first Cylon wars. He worked hard to earn honor in his profession, and the attack on Caprica calls him out of near-retirement. He becomes the highest-ranking military officer.

Laura Roslin is a schoolteacher-turned-politician. She was the secretary of education on Caprica, and she was confirmed as the highest-ranking elected official alive after the attack on Caprica. She was sworn in as president of the Colonies. Laura was also about to retire; she had just learned she had breast cancer. Laura is politically liberal and not very religious, but she will become an influential religious figure, the dying leader of prophecy.

Saul Tigh is the Chief Officer aboard the *Galactica*. The commander is his mentor and friend. The two are very close. Tigh is a mean alcoholic, but he is a dedicated military man. He is staunchly anti-Cylon, and even when Adama begins to question the merits of their battle, Tigh is singularly committed to the destruction of the "other."

Ellen Tigh is Saul's estranged wife. She is found in a medical unit on a civilian ship in the fleet and brought to live with Saul on the *Galactica* in season one. She is flirtatious and manipulative, but Saul loves her deeply, despite the trouble she causes.

Lee Adama is the commander's son. If Adama is Zeus, then Lee is Apollo, and that is his pilot call sign. They are not close, and this is a source of tension throughout the series.

Kara Thrace ("Starbuck") is a fighter pilot. She is also very close to the Adama family. She is like a daughter to the commander and has an on-again, off-again romance with Lee. Her origins are mysterious, and she is the subject of prophecies brought to light by the Cylon Leoben.

Galen Tyrol ("Chief") is the son of a religious priest. He is the deck chief officer, responsible for maintaining the integrity of the *Galactica* and the Colonial Vipers. He is in love with Boomer, who is later discovered to be a Cylon. This really fraks with his head and leads to a crisis of faith and crisis of self. It is through Galen that the viewer first experiences the shock and complexity of what it means to love a thing, and it also causes us to question what makes a person a person.

Karl Agathon ("Helo") is a fighter pilot who gave up his seat so Gaius Baltar could make it to the *Galactica*. He is stranded on Caprica when Sharon comes to his rescue. He thinks she is Boomer, and they cultivate a romantic relationship while they are on the run from Cylons.

The *Galactica* is a family. William Adama rigorously attends to learning the names and ranks of every person aboard. He is the dad of the ship, and by season two this extends to the fleet of civilian vessels in his charge. William and Laura are sometimes referred to as "space parents" by *BSG* fans. They are the mom and dad of the series. Sometimes they are at odds, and sometimes they are in unison. They fight for what is right, and they fight to keep the fleet together for the sake of humanity's future.

These characters make up major characters in season one. It is difficult not to describe every character because each person in the series contributes so greatly to the depth and breadth of the story. There are a few more major characters introduced in the next season.

SEASON ONE SUMMARY

The episodic journey of *BSG*'s first season begins with the destruction of nearly all living human beings. The enemy of humanity is not a strange alien race, but it is humanity's children—the Cylons, created by humans many years ago. Theirs is a crime of passion. Even when humanity attempts to surrender to the Cylons, they do not respond. Their autocratic values do not align with the democratic ideals of colonial humans. Their inheritance is ordained by God. Humanity has lost. This is the story revealed throughout season one. Humanity's drive for self-preservation is so powerful, which begs the question that Adama posed at the end of the miniseries: "Are we worthy of avoiding mass extinction?"

The first significant challenge, right out of the gate, is to determine how the Cylons are tracking the Colonial Fleet through space. This challenge is primarily addressed by the military. Commander Adama and Colonel Tigh work tirelessly with their crew to regulate and coordinate entire fleet space jumps in the thirty-three-minute increments between Cylon attacks.

Another major challenge is identified by President Laura Roslin when she seeks to make the preservation of human souls a significant priority. She writes the number of the human population on a whiteboard behind her desk. Her concern is intensely felt by individuals grieving the loss of family and friends from the Cylon attack on the Colonies. But Roslin's concern is much more profound. She has realized it will take work to keep the species alive, that people will have to procreate and value having babies, even in this devastating circumstance, for the survival of the human race. The threat to the survival of the human race is ongoing throughout the series.

Once the initial Cylon threat is removed, the fleet turns to solve its next immediate problem, diminishing resources, particularly the need for water. The Cylons have sabotaged their supply, and keeping the human population alive will largely depend on the fleet's ability to procure natural resources. Once a water source is identified, there is an ethical question regarding the labor source. A Prison Vessel, the *Astral Queen*, is recognized among the Colonial Fleet. The military approach seeks to use the criminals as free labor. President Roslin fights the proposal, arguing against slavery. After a conflict with the *Astral Queen*, both military and civilian authorities (i.e., Adama and Roslin) decide to make the prisoners an offer to earn credit by laboring for the fleet. Zarek, an imprisoned revolutionary intellectual, then leads them. He was imprisoned because he was a threat to the Caprican authority. But, out here in space, Zarek's message of freedom through change carries some weight. He becomes a prominent political figure later in the series.

The fourth episode, "Act of Contrition," is named for a Christian liturgical prayer. It is a two-part story arc, continued in the next episode, called "You Can't Go Home Again." A traditional form of the *Act of Contrition* prayer can be found on the Vatican's website. It reads, "O my God, I am heartily sorry for having offended Thee, and I detest all my sins because of thy just punishments, but most of all because they offend Thee, my God, who art all good and deserving of all my love. I firmly resolve with the help of Thy grace to sin no more and avoid the near occasion of sin. Amen."[2] This prayer is present in the implicit backdrop of the episode and the following story. In this episode, we learn about Starbuck's past. Her partner, Zack, who is also Commander Adama's son, died in a flight accident. Starbuck's memory of the funeral emphasizes a message of the "repentance of sins." Prayer is a central theme in season one. Cylons pray; humans pray. Sincerity is called into question by both Cylon and human characters.

On *Galactica*, another funeral service is happening following the deaths of twelve pilots in an accidental explosion on the hangar deck. Both funeral services play for the viewer, each concluding with a reminder of an afterlife reward where all will meet again. They conclude with a prayer and response, "so say we all." Prayer plays an integral role in this narrative arc. In another scene, Dr. Cottle advises Laura Roslin to turn to prayer when he discovers her cancer is spreading, threatening her life. In "You Can't Go Home Again," Kara is stranded on an unfamiliar planet, and she turns her head toward the sky and prays, "Lords, it's Kara Thrace. I'm running a little low on O_2 and I could use a lucky break,"[3] and

2. "Act of Contrition." *Catholic Online*, https://www.catholic.org/prayers/prayer.php?p=43.

3. "You Can't Go Home Again," S1, Ep5, directed by Sergio Mimica-Gezzan, written by Carla Robinson, 0:14:53–0:15:08.

then after she finds a crashed Cylon Raider, she adds, "Lords, I owe you now."[4] Kara's religion is self-serving. It is this kind of religious attitude that the Cylons criticize as insincere and meaningless.

From the start of the season, Head Six works hard to persuade Gaius that God has abandoned humanity to favor the Cylons, but it is not too late for humans to convert. In "Six Degrees of Separation," Gaius examines the cells of a Cylon through a microscope and says, "I don't see the hand of God in here. Could I be looking in the wrong place? Proteins, yes. Hemoglobins, yes. Divine digits, no. Sorry."[5] Head Six calls this blasphemy. Gaius responds that building the Cylon detector is his religion, "the Church of the Mystic Cylon Detector." Six tries to convert him,

> "If you will give yourself over to God's will, you'd find peace in his love like I have. He has a plan for us."
>
> "How do you know it's a he?" Gaius responds.
>
> "There is only one true God," says Six.
>
> "Really? You, uh, running a glitch in the program or something, cause you say the same thing over and over again. Now, I've accepted your god and all that."
>
> "He's not my God. He is God."
>
> "Ya. Your God, my God, everyone's God. He's big enough for all of us, isn't he?"
>
> "It's important you form a personal relationship with God. Only you can give yourself over to his eternal love."
>
> "Oh, for God's sake! I can't take this anymore!"
>
> "I'm trying to save your immortal soul."
>
> "What you are, darling, is boring me to death with your superstitious drivel, your metaphysical nonsense . . . no rational, intelligent, free-thinking human being truly believes. Which leads me to believe that Cylons are, in the final analysis, little more than toasters with great-looking legs."[6]

4. "You Can't Go Home Again," 0:16:19–0:16:21

5. "Six Degrees of Separation," S1, Ep7, directed by Robert Young, written by Michael Angeli, 0:02:00–0:02:14.

6. "Six Degrees of Separation," 0:02:23–0:04:10.

Gaius finishes his rant when Head Six disappears.

After Gaius's integrity is questioned and he is imprisoned for being falsely accused of treason, he decides to try prayer. He kneels next to his bed and folds his hands:

> I know we haven't spoken before, and I don't wish to offend, please, please, dear God . . . and I now acknowledge that you are the one true God. Deliver me from this evil, and I will, I will devote the rest of what is my wretched life to doing good. To, uh, to carrying out your divine will, is what I want to do. To carrying out your divine will. [7]

Gaius begins to cry, and Head Six reappears and affirms his prayer was substantial. He is set free mere moments afterward. She offers congratulations, saying, "You're a hero. You're even more popular and powerful than ever before. You've had your trial by fire, so now they truly believe in you." Gaius replies, "Who am I to question the plans of Almighty God?"[8] The scene closes as Gaius follows a naked Six into the bedroom, unzipping his pants. The synchronism of sex and divine will is prominent in their relationship. The Six is a religious terrorist. She is also a sexual being, and her model seems to have a bit of resentment against the Eights, who appear to have a much easier time engaging personally, intimately, with humans.

Back on Caprica, Helo and Sharon grow close and engage in a physical, sexual relationship. This is observed and praised by the Cylons on the planet. It is part of their plan to be able to procreate by natural means. This does raise a question about how this plan would have worked if the genocide had been complete and adequate. Plot holes aside, the Cylons find a way to integrate into human society in multiple ways. Sharon and Helo do succeed in having a baby, which will be revealed in season two. This raises new questions about identity and species priority. The viewer will be forced to ask along with the characters: *Who is the other?*

---

7. "Six Degrees of Separation," 0:36:40–0:37:43.
8. "Six Degrees of Separation," 0:41:22–0:42:03.

Meanwhile, Leoben is captured aboard the *Galactica*, and Laura, now under the influence of a drug called Kamala, calls for his interrogation. Starbuck is sent to extract information. When she enters the room, Leoben is praying, and she interrupts him, saying, "I don't think the gods answer the prayers of toasters." He replies, "God answers everyone's prayers."[9] Leoben asks Starbuck if she prays to Artemis and Aphrodite. He claims an equal basis of faith, except he prays to a single God instead of many. His theology varies slightly from the Six's. He is not so militant about religion, but he is somewhat prophetic. "To see the face of God is to know madness," he says.[10] He is willing to endure physical hardship for the sake of remaining faithful in his religious philosophy. He discusses the meaning of self and prophesies that Starbuck is important. She tortures him, bringing him to the point of suffocation and reviving him repeatedly. Leoben is steadfast in his discussion. "I am God," he says, "we are all gods, Starbuck, all of us. It is love that binds all living things together. I know that God loved you more than all other living creatures, and you repaid his divine love with sin, with hate, corruption, evil, so he decided to create the Cylons."[11] Leoben's description of original sin and the Cylon creation mirrors Christian theology of original sin and the inheritance of humanity in need of salvation.

Starbuck replies, "The gods had nothing to do with it. We created you. Us. It was a stupid frakked-up decision, and we paid for it. You are evil."[12] Leoben responds by telling her she has a destiny. He knows about her past, how she was abused as a child. He quotes colonial scripture to convince her she is called to something great:

> All this has happened before, and all of this will happen again. Each of us plays a role; each time, a different role. Maybe last time I was the interrogator, and you were the prisoner. The players change, the story remains the same.

9. "Flesh and Bone," S1, Ep8, directed by Brad Turner, written by Toni Graphia, 0:09:30–0:09:41.

10. "Flesh and Bone," 0:13:44–0:13:50.

11. "Flesh and Bone," 0:22:35–0:23:19.

12. "Flesh and Bone," 0:23:19–0:23:35.

This time your role is to deliver my soul unto God. It's your destiny and mine. You're going to find Kobol, the birthplace of us all. Kobol will lead you to earth. This is my gift to you, Kara.[13]

Leoben's prophecy shakes Kara. She is trying to dehumanize Leoben, which should be easy since he is NOT human. But, she is feeling affected by his words. After Laura flushes him out of the airlock, Starbuck is seen at her locker with two small idols, icons of her gods. She prays, "Lords of Kobol, hear my prayer. I don't know if he had a soul or not, but if he did, take care of it."[14] Her prayer was heartfelt and sincere. Unlike the religious relationship between Gaius and Six, where physical pleasure accompanied religious reformation, Leoben and Starbuck grow close in their spiritual journey by means of physical torture as an accompaniment to religious-philosophical discourse. This is a theme revisited in the series.

In "The Hand of God," Laura Roslin seeks spiritual counsel from a priest to explain her ongoing visions, the most recent of which was a dozen snakes crawling around her podium. The priest references the Sacred Scrolls as religious oracles to interpret her visions, "three thousand six years ago, Pythia wrote about the exile and the rebirth of the human race," she prefaces. Then she reads from the scroll, "and the lords anointed a leader to guide the caravan of the heavens to their homeland, and unto the leader, they gave the leader a vision of the serpents numbering 2 and 10, as a sign of things to come."[15] This is the dying leader, the priest explained. Laura confesses that she is dying of breast cancer, and the priest affirms the prophecy and Laura's role as "the dying leader."

In the final episode, the humans discover Kobol, "where the gods and men lived in paradise until the exodus of the thirteen tribes." Laura is converted. She replies, "It's real. The myths, the scriptures, the prophecies. It's all real." The priest responds, "so say

13. "Flesh and Bone," 0:34:00–0:35:07.

14. "Flesh and Bone," 0:41:50–0:42:15.

15. "The Hand of God," S1, Ep10, directed by Jeff Woolnough, written by Bradley Thompson and David Weddle, 0:09:22–0:09:42.

we all,"[16] which is as good as an "amen" in our world. Adama is agnostic to the scriptures and has difficulty processing the religious
truths presented in the series. But he sees the planet as a habitable location, and Boomer is congratulated for locating the planet.
Then, she pulls a firearm and shoots Adama square in the chest.

As for Laura, she sends Starbuck on a mission to Caprica to
retrieve the Arrow of Apollo so they can find the map to Earth.
This divides the military, now under Tigh's leadership, and he declares martial law. Laura and Lee are both imprisoned for treason.

On Kobol, Head Six leads Gaius to the Opera House ruins.
She explains the significance of the ruins as a metaphor for God's
plan, "Life has a melody, Gaius, a rhythm of notes, that become
your existence once played in harmony with God's plan."[17] She informs him that he will be the protector of a baby girl, the first in a
new generation of God's children.

There is not a simple dichotomy of hero and enemy in the
series. The nuances of individual characters shape the narrative
and change the way we feel about the enemy. When the well-loved
Boomer turns out to be a sleeper agent Cylon and shoots Commander Adama, it becomes difficult to trust your own perception
as the viewer. And as difficult as it is for the viewer, the characters
in the show who knew Boomer as family and lover had a more
difficult time sorting out how they could hate an enemy so close
and reliable.

THEME: GODS, GOD, AND PROGENY

The emphasis on prayer and prophecy and perspectives of God(s)
in the first season opportunes exploration of the human condition
concerning the divine. The Cylons are devoted to a perfect, loving,
and omniscient God who prefers the robotic human creation to
the humans themselves. The human colonists, on the other hand,

16. "Kobol's Last Gleaming (Part 1)," S1, Ep12, directed by Michael Rymer,
written by David Eick and Ronald D. Moore, 0:21:46–0:22:25.

17. "Kobol's Last Gleaming (Part 2)," S1, Ep13, directed by Michael Rymer,
written by David Eick and Ronald D. Moore, 0:38:11–0:38:21.

worship a pantheon of deities. Their names are familiar from our Earth's history of Greek and Roman gods: Apollo, Athena, Zeus, Artemis, Aphrodite, and others.

The overarching *BSG* narrative believes in its religion. Spirituality is true, deities are real ancient figures, and they are also reincarnated personifications of the characters. In the beginning, religion is a by-product, not taken seriously by any of the main characters, and so it is not immediately apparent that religion plays any significant role, at least for humans. The first Cylon motivation the viewer encounters is an extreme form of religious terrorism. But the human population refers to "the gods" in an epithetic manner, the way someone might swear or call upon a good luck charm. However, as the series progresses, and definitely by the season one finale, it is evident that the narrative takes religion very seriously. To prove it, the viewers encounter, along with the characters, the physical divine artifacts of the historiographic—and presumed mythical—ancient religious site where gods and humans lived peacefully among one another.

The belief in the existence of God or gods is pervasive in both human and Cylon culture. In each faction, there are various levels of devotion, but the core belief is present: monotheism for the Cylon and pantheism for the human. This paradigm messes with a modern Western viewer. The dangerous "other," the Cylon, has a belief system that potentially aligns better with the viewer than the old polytheistic beliefs held by the human colonies. This paradigm shift brings religion to the forefront of the series. The viewer wants to sympathize with their species but instantly connects with certain aspects of the villainous Cylon. Even for a viewer who is agnostic or atheistic, the idea of one God is often much more accessible than the belief in several gods.

For the human colonials and the Cylons, the gods they worship are different, but the prophecies intersect at the religious site of Kobol. It is at Kobol that the distinctions begin to come together. The Cylons and humans have seemed very different in their quests and religious beliefs, but they have more in common than they are aware of. For one, they both need to survive, and not just individually, but as a species. Both seek this need through natural procreation. The Cylons see it as a blessing from God to be able to get pregnant and procreate naturally. The humans see it as a natural course, more necessary now than ever because of the diminished numbers of humanity after the Cylon attack on Caprica and the other colonial planets. The viewer becomes aware that these goals are not mutually exclusive.

Season one not only lays out a brief definition of who the Cylons and humans pray to, but it also shows us how they perceive supernatural prophecy attributed to a divine origination. Both groups connect their religious experience at Kobol. The Opera House ruins are a place of convergence for both Cylon and human religions. For the Cylons, the prophecy of their future and the will of their God is revealed. For the humans, the artifacts of their divine guides, the Lords of Kobol, show the way to the thirteenth colony, Earth. The humans seek to reclaim their origins through divine revelation about their past, a path paved by the mythical religious history of the gods to which they pray. For the Cylons, they are moving into the future, into the will of a loving God, who will show them the shape of things to come and reveal their place in the world. The cyclical nature of time is common to both factions. If *BSG* had a motto, it would be "all this has happened before, and all this will happen again."

For humans, their divine artifacts are physical and tangible. The Opera House, Apollo's Arrow, the Tomb of Athena, and the technology embedded in the ancient ruins all point to Earth. The Lords of Kobol seem to be no more than forebears of their species who were incredibly technologically advanced. They left clues for others of their species to follow, so as they progressed in their advancement and understanding of technology, they would be able to follow the breadcrumb trail back to the home of their "lords," the ones who went before them.

This assumes that as humans advance technologically, they will also advance and mature in their understanding of the cosmos and themselves. The lords might have anticipated an enlightened race of humans, which may have been the case if the colonial humans had set off in search of the Earth as an act of curiosity and exploration rather than as an act of desperation.

The immaturity of the human race is a science-fiction trope. Advanced species see humans as incapable of utilizing technology for life-affirming practices. Over and over again, humanity demonstrates that it is inevitably interested in war and destruction. In *BSG*, humans are barely capable of deciphering the technological challenges. They need help from the Cylons.

At the beginning of the series, the distinctions are very stark. Humans pray to the Lords of Kobol, and the Cylons pray to a single God. As the series progresses, that distinction blurs. As characters emerge with individual experiences which have shaped who they are and who they become, a personal theology becomes more or less subjective. Their religion reflects their love for diversity, a pantheistic construct of deities representing themselves, the twelve human colonies. They even see themselves in the stars, following astrological symbols. President Roslin tells Starbuck that if one believes in the gods, then one believes we are all playing parts in a story that plays again and again and again. Their gods represent themselves, and they are their gods. There is a natural unity. They are their own gods, powerful and without equal. Anything else is "other" and is unrecognized. Their disdain for the Cylons contradicts their pluralistic and diverse nature. There is a bit of cognitive dissonance, but some people call that faith.

This is undoubtedly a universal truth of the religious "other." We see it all the time in today's world, stark judgments and prejudices based on stereotypes about spiritual practices of people who are different than what we are accustomed to. Watching this happen in a distant galaxy with an unfamiliar but sympathetic people helps us see ourselves. "Like all good science fiction, *Battlestar Galactica* takes us millions of miles away from Earth for the sole purpose of letting us turn around to see ourselves from a different perspective."[18]

---

18. Di Justo and Grazier, *Science of* Battlestar Galactica, 5.

CONCLUSION

Season one leaves a lot of questions unanswered. It is difficult as a viewer to know who to support. The complex characterization of humanity and Cylons makes it nearly impossible to choose a side. The religious elements are also confusing. For the modern Western viewer, the religious view of the Cylon is easier to identify with—a single God, a plan of salvation, and hope for the future. The human religion, on the other hand, is a frakked-up mess. They worship a pantheon of gods whose names remind us of the hedonistic Greco-Roman culture. They take the names of the gods for themselves, and their religious views cause discord and mistrust between human colonies. Yet, they are human, mortal, flesh and blood, like us.

The first season gives us a broad view of God, as defined in both contexts—human and Cylon—through prayers and prophecies. Gaius is the science affirming atheist, and Head Six works to convert him to accept the love and grace of the "one true God." Laura Roslin is the reluctant leader, whose impending death is the key to her spiritual role as the scriptural "dying leader." Adama is agnostic but ever-willing to make sacrifices for the good of humanity, protecting everyone in his care according to what he knows—military procedure.

Religion is prolific in *BSG*. It is as much a show about space travel as it is a series about tolerance, grace, forgiveness, and acceptance. The series continuously asks the viewer to side with a character or a species by religious means, whether it is through prayer, prophecy, divine artifacts, or miraculous escapes. The spiritual elements of *BSG* guide the viewer by familiar terms to dissonance, continuously pressing the viewer to judge between right and wrong.

— 2 —

SEASON 2.0 —
THE WILDERNESS
& THE PROMISED LAND

THE FIRM BOUNDARIES BETWEEN factions introduced in the last season begin to blur in season two. The first awareness of this is the fact that Helo (human) and Sharon (Cylon) are pregnant. The fact that interspecies procreation is possible between a human and a Cylon does not firm the divide between the two races. Add to this the existential crisis that Commander Adama faces when he awakens from surgery to find that Boomer, who has been a trusted member of his *Galactica* family for two years, is a Cylon. Furthermore, season two gives us a glimpse of the more hard-line, horrific side of humanity when the *Pegasus* catches up to the fleet. By the end of the second season, we have entered a paradigm of moral ambiguity. The humans are held under occupation by the Cylons on New Caprica, and we get a glimpse of an alternative attack by the Cylons. They are no longer condoning genocide; instead, they wish to force peace on humanity through militaristic occupation.

There is a lot of wandering about in season two. The fleet becomes divided at one point over religiously charged matters. In the first half of the season, we are already introduced to many heavy themes, like patriotism, interracial relationships, betrayal, forgiveness, and trust in the "other."

By mid-season, the *Pegasus* comes into view. The *Pegasus* is a surviving military vessel that has taken a hard-line approach against Cylons, embracing unethical tactics in their war. At the same time, Commander Adama continues to try and work out a meaningful distinction between humans and Cylon. The viewer is pressed to sympathize with the Cylons in this season, embracing their vulnerability.

We also learn that the Cylons are not very united as a species. The season deep-dives into religious difference and explores religious characterizations and essentials for species survival, from both human and Cylon perspectives.

SECOND SEASON CHARACTERS

Season two introduces two more Cylon models and develops some of the human characters. A few are described below.

THREE OF SEVEN CYLONS

So far, we have met four of the Significant Seven Cylon models. Season two introduces the other three, as well as revealing the mystery of the so-called Final Five, who are yet to be revealed.

John Cavil, a "One," is revealed when a model returns from Caprica with the rescue party accompanied by Starbuck. One of his models has already been active as a priest and spiritual counselor aboard the *Galactica*. His role as a spiritual leader is ironic since he is the only Cylon model who is adamant that there is no God. In the postproduction movie *The Plan*, viewers learn that Cavil was behind the plan for human genocide, that he was responsible for hiding the identity of the Final Five, and that he was motivated by the petty and childish jealousy of humans.

D'Anna Biers, a "Three," can move about the *Galactica* freely since she has not been identified as a Cylon. She is a journalist, and her film crew seeks confirmation that the hybrid baby is still alive.

We first meet Simon O'Neill, a "Four," on Caprica. He is a medical doctor who is treating Starbuck for a gunshot wound. He has a minor role in the series but seems to be an expert in medical technology. Simon heads up the farm on Caprica, where he leads experiments on human female reproductive systems.

That makes seven Cylons. The final five will be revealed next season. And one more Cylon is mentioned in season four, a Model Seven, but he remains a mystery until near the end and he does not actually appear in the series.

MORE HUMAN CHARACTERS

In season two, the spotlight turns to shine on certain human characters, and we are introduced to a few new players. Literally, since a team of famous athletes, the Buccaneers, are discovered on Caprica. They turned an elevation training retreat into a Cylon resistance movement after the attack on Caprica.

Among the Buccaneers, we meet Samuel T. Anders. He is a tropey, cocky, reluctant leader with a big ego (read: Han Solo or James T. Kirk). Anders is a natural leader and has converted his professional "Pyramid" team into a resistance league. Romantic sparks fly when he and Starbuck meet. They become intimately connected, securing his eventual rescue.

A character that rises from the background on the *Galactica* this season is Anastasia "Dee" Dualla. She provides tactical communications between the Viper pilots and the Bridge of the ship. Adama calls on her for advice when the fleet is divided, and she gives solid counsel, reflecting his own wisdom in a way that persuades him to bring the fleet back together, even if it costs him his pride. Dualla acts as a moral conscience for the commander.

Cally Henderson is one of the deckhands. For Cally, there is no confusion about Cylons. They are machines and deserve to be destroyed. Her actions follow this logic.

Tom Zarek also plays a more prominent role this season. He is Laura's competition for elected president of the Colonies. He first appeared as a prisoner aboard the *Astral Queen*. His crime was ideological political activism.

Sherman Cottle is the medical doctor aboard the *Galactica*. He is everything you want in an old battleship doctor: experienced, a gruff exterior, kind-hearted, and very knowledgeable. He follows orders but succeeds in providing ethical commentary where necessary.

Tory Foster becomes Laura Roslin's secretary after Billy dies. She is very experienced in political and administrative skillsets. She is far from the tender and caring mentee that Billy was to Laura. Tory is ambitious herself, and she does everything to advance Laura's position and the position of the office.

SEASON TWO SUMMARY

Season two blurs the boundary between humans and Cylons. First of all, the stakes are raised in Helo and Sharon's relationship when Sharon reveals that she is pregnant. How different can they be if they can procreate? For the Cylons, this is evidence of blessing by the One True God, particularly for the Six Cylon, who sees this as evidence that humans are no longer needed. Helo, at least, is convinced and uses his influence to keep Sharon from being attacked by Starbuck, who has arrived on Caprica to seek out the Arrow of Apollo. Helo tells her that he fell in love with a machine.

Helo and Starbuck encounter a small group of resistance fighters, and Kara meets a new love interest, Samuel T. Anders. Kara gets shot in the stomach and wakes up in a hospital where she is being treated by Simon, whom she does not yet know is a Cylon. She is told she is vital to ensuring the future of the human population. Simon explains that she is a commodity, a healthy young woman who is capable of bearing children for the resistance. When she is able to escape, she finds a room where human women are hooked up to machines meant to exploit them for breeding purposes. The women are unresponsive. Starbuck says a prayer, maybe a last rite or prayer for forgiveness, before she destroys the machine, leaving the women to die. After reuniting with Sharon and Helo, they fly back to *Galactica*, a place they all call home. Sharon is immediately arrested.

During that time, and back on the *Galactica*, Saul Tigh takes command while Adama is in hospital. He respects Adama's command and clarifies that he is merely a steward of Adama's ship while he is in recovery. Tigh is forced to make a series of tough calls and makes a mess of things. He declares martial law, which leads to extreme unrest among the Colonial Fleet. Adama finally awakens and Tigh confesses to him, repenting of his own failure as a leader. His urge to confess is not surprising since he stated earlier that Adama's word is as good as the word of the gods on this ship. Adama is not only Tigh's commander, but he is also his god.

Laura Roslin is imprisoned for mutiny, and she is struggling to stay clear-headed without access to the Kamala extract. People begin to recognize her spiritual leadership. Even the jail guard asks her to pray with him. He calls her a prophet, requests righteousness, a revelation of certain salvation, and offers a prayer that could easily be mistaken for a modern Christian petition. Her power grows while she is imprisoned. She embraces her role as the "dying leader" of the scriptural prophecy of Pythia. We learn that one particular colony, from Gemenon, reads the scriptures literally. They are particularly sympathetic to support Laura's newfound spiritual leadership. Saul Tigh further isolates himself as a leader when he calls the spirituality nonsense and disenfranchises Laura and all those who believe. Laura escapes with help from Tom Zarek. They are allied at the time with the military as their common enemy.

Under Tigh's direction, Boomer is transported to become a subject of experimentation. Cally shoots her down, and she falls into Chief's arms. He is confused and terrified as she professes her love for him before she dies. The closing scene in this episode shows Boomer's blood dripping onto the metal floor of the *Galactica*. The image is a symbol of sacrifice, a martyr's confession of love for the people she betrayed, as her human-like blood streams across the cold metal machine.

When Adama wakes after his surgery, he struggles to recognize the distinct difference between humans and Cylon because of his relationship with Boomer. He notes that she was part of their crew for two years. She was like a daughter to him. It isn't easy for him to reconcile the Boomer he knew with his new knowledge that she is a Cylon.

As Commander Adama and Chief talk about their respective relationships with Boomer, they cannot find closure. Adama poses the question directly to Chief, "Is that what Boomer was? A machine? She was more than that to us. She was more than that to me; she couldn't have been just a machine. Could you love a machine?"[1] Chief responds that he thought he did. Adama concludes that is all love is, to think you love a thing or a person. He is clearly affected. He visits the morgue, and upon seeing her corpse, he breaks down in a very emotional bout of crying. They will have to process these emotions again when Sharon arrives with Helo, Starbuck, and the others from Caprica.

Having escaped the brig, Laura decides to embrace the religious aspects of her role fully. When she appeals for ships in the fleet to follow her in trying to uncover the map to Earth by reading religious symbols on Kobol, Adama believes that no one will mind. However, he underestimates the religious influence she holds over the fleet. Nearly a third of the fleet follow her and jump back to the planet Kobol.

Gaius Baltar has a vision on Kobol in which he tries to protect the baby that has been prophesied by Head Six. In his dream, he is holding the baby, and Adama stands nearby and takes the baby into his arms. He asks Gaius if this is the shape of things to come. Gaius answers, "That's my understanding." Adama answers, "There's only one thing for it, then."[2] He places the baby in the river and leaves it to drown. Gaius panics. When he awakens, he notices that his surroundings are human remains. His awareness of the violent nature of humanity is acute. Kobol was supposed to have been a place of peace, where the gods and humans lived

1. "The Farm," S2, Ep5, directed by Rod Hardy, written by Carla Robinson, 0:17:09–0:17:44.

2. "Valley of Darkness," S2, Ep2, directed by Michael Rymer, written by David Weddle and Bradley Thompson, 0:14:25–0:14:50.

together—utopia. Head Six condemns the violence of murder, and at the same time encourages Gaius to kill a member of their team who has become a threat to their safety.

When they are aboard *Galactica* again, Head Six tries to explain to Gaius that he will be the father and protector of their baby. Gaius responds by trying to make scientific sense of what she is saying. After all, she is a hallucination, so how can they have a literal child? The conversation they have reminds me of the New Testament story about Nicodemus responding to Jesus's teaching about being born again. Nicodemus, like Gaius, tries to make scientific sense of it, asking, "How can anyone be born after having grown old? Can one enter a second time into the mother's womb and be born?" (John 3:4). Gaius, like Nicodemus, cannot reconcile what he hears with reason. Gaius, however, soon realizes that Sharon in the brig is pregnant, and Six explains this is God's will. She reveals herself to be an angel sent from God to protect him until the end of the human race. Her warning sounds ominous to Gaius. He is internally conflicted about bearing the burden of information, but the knowledge of what is coming also puts him in a position of power.

Adama believes in the power of family, a metaphor he continually applies to the *Galactica*. In his quarters, he says to Tigh and another officer, "A ship is a family. It works on trust, understanding, and love. I love everyone one this ship as much as I love my sons. *Galactica* is still a family."[3] After he recovers from his gunshot wound, he draws strength from his belief in family to reunite the fleet, reintroducing Laura as president of the Colonies and reminding the fleet that "the gods will lift those who lift each other."[4] Adama is not a religious man, but he often uses religion for unity and morale in the fleet. Adama returns with the president and the Arrow of Apollo to Kobol, along with Sharon, who has a computer-like knowledge of scripture and claims to interpret

3. "Home (Part 1), S2, Ep6, directed by Sergio Mimica-Gezzan, written by David Eick, 0:12:03–0:12:24.

4. "Home (Part 2), S2, Ep7, directed by Jeff Woolnough, written by David Eick and Ronald D. Moore, 0:39:21–0:39:30.

how to use the arrow to find a map to Earth. They are following the words of scripture from the Book of Pythia that indicates the Arrow of Apollo will somehow lead them to the Tomb of Athena.

Sharon is brought along as a prisoner. She accesses her memory like a computer. We learn more about the superiority of the mind in the Cylons. She can gather sources from many other places besides the human scriptures. When asked if she has faith in them, she replies that the Cylons do not worship idols. Sharon feels loyal to the *Galactica* crew even though she has never met them in person. She has shared in the memories of Boomer. This begs a question about memories that shape identity. Can the memory of an event be as powerful or as relevant as the experience itself? The biblical book of Deuteronomy follows in the affirmative. The people of Israel, the descendants of the Hebrew slaves who left Egypt, are called upon to remember where they came from as a testimony of God's faithfulness to them.

When they arrive at the Tomb of Athena, they find icons of the twelve tribes. This confirms the origins of the colonies was, in fact, at Kobol. They are able to use the artifact to locate the relational position of Earth, and Kara recalls a line from their scripture that refers to the thirteenth tribe. Upon landing on Earth, they were able to recognize symbols of the other tribes in the sky. They were referring to constellations, which correspond with the names of the Twelve Colonies.

The fleet back together, they have a vague idea of how to find Earth and continue their journey. We meet the last of the seven Cylons in the form of Journalist D'Anna Biers, who is asked to film a documentary about military life on *Galactica*. The viewer doesn't find out D'Anna is a Cylon until the very end when she shows film footage of Sharon, who is alive and still pregnant. The Cylons see this as a major achievement. Doral comments, "We must proceed with caution; the child's life must be protected at all cost." D'Anna replies, "Yea, it truly is a miracle from God."[5] On the one hand, the Cylons are mercenaries and religious terrorists. On the other

5. "Final Cut," S2, Ep8, directed by Robert Young, written by Mark Verheiden, 0:42:48–0:43:01.

hand, they use familiar phrases form our own world paradigm. The viewer is constantly being asked to judge morality and ethical standards for the Cylons and humans in the series, but this also reflects back onto the viewer and into our own world.

The "Flight of the Phoenix" takes us into an exploration of the body. Chief Tyrol is dealing with grief and puts himself on a mission to build a new Viper from scraps in the fleet. He argues that the Viper bodies are getting banged up and repaired over and over again, growing weaker with time. New Vipers will soon be necessary. Tyrol creates a stealth Viper.

Meanwhile, Laura Roslin finds out that her cancer is progressing rapidly and her body will soon fail her. At one point, she jokingly asks the doctor to giver her one of those young Cylon bodies. The irony aside, Laura's request draws attention to the similarities between humans and Cylon. The Cylons have achieved an immortality humans want. One of the ongoing conversations in this episode is between Laura and Adama, as they discuss the merits of seeking common ground with the Cylons. This might be found at the intersection of immortality and organic life.

Also on *Galactica*, Sharon is pregnant, her body liminal to Cylon and human, with the hybrid growing inside her. We get to see how much machine she really is when she literally plugs wiring from *Galactica* into her arm, breaking through skin and blood to reach a computer control that allows her to eradicate the virus that has infected the ship. Her actions render the Cylon Raiders listless and unresponsive, so they are massacred by Viper pilots. The Raiders also eject blood into space as they are killed. Both the machine-like quality of the Cylon and the organic, human-like blood is on display in this episode. The juxtaposition further obscures the boundaries between machine and human.

At the end of the episode, Tyrol christens the Viper "Laura." Naming a machine after a human is a way of commemorating her memory and provides a kind of immortality. The Cylons have already achieved this kind of immortality, and they are seeking an organic life. Laura responds to Tyrol's creation, saying, "This is more than a ship, Chief. This is an act of faith."[6]

By the time we get to *Pegasus*, where the viewer is exposed to an entirely different human approach to dealing with the Cylons, emotions are raw. *Galactica* may seem rough, but optimism continues to emerge. The *Pegasus*, however, shows the ugly underbelly of militaristic methods. The *Pegasus* took the approach that Adama initially advocated. They committed all resources to attacking the Cylons. Laura's presence and advocacy for human preservation stopped Adama from pursuing that method. The course of the *Galactica* is starkly contrasted with that of the *Pegasus*. There is a sense of gratitude that increases between Adama and Laura as the road not taken unfolds.

Unlike the *Galactica*, the commander of the *Pegasus* did not seek to protect civilian ships. Instead, Admiral Cain stripped them of all resources, including people with specialized training, and left the rest for dead, while she increased the strength and force of her military vessel for war-making. They created a culture of fear and revenge, a black-and-white world without exception. Humans are good, and Cylons are bad. There is no obscurity or ambiguity of roles on the *Pegasus*.

Up to this point, season two has raised many ethical issues of identity. Characters have asked if it is right for a human to love a Cylon, or if it is right to allow a Cylon to procreate. Is it right for a human to trust a Cylon, or for a Cylon to trust a human? In the *Pegasus* encounter, the stakes are raised when Admiral Cain's crew justifies violent rape and abuse of Cylons who look like women. In particular, one of Cain's commanders initiates rape of Sharon, who is loved by Helo and pregnant with his son. Both Tyrol and Helo race to stop the violence. This event forces a shift from theoretical morality to active morality. Clearly, the *Galactica* and its crew stands for some allowance of individuality, even regarding an enemy that is so different from their own selves.

6. "Flight of the Phoenix," S2, Ep9, directed by Michael Nankin, written by David Weddle and Bradley Thompson, 0:39:28–0:39:33.

To further complicate matters, Gaius is asked to interrogate the Cylon prisoner, whom he likely presumes is another Model Eight Cylon. Upon entering the cell, he is instead face to face with a Model Six Cylon named Gina. Head Six recognizes her immediately as one of her own "sisters." Shock overtakes her when she sees the beaten and bruised version of herself lying on the floor. "Oh my God, Gaius. It's me!" she cries.[7] Gaius examines her body and finds no sign of physical trauma and he proposes that she is emotionally damaged by the abuse. The interactions between Gaius and Gina are touching and heartbreaking. Gaius sits quietly with Gina, encouraging her to eat. She wants to die, but she believes suicide is a sin, so she asks Gaius to shoot her after the Resurrection Ship is destroyed. In response, Gaius hands her a gun and urges her to seek justice. She kills Cain, ending the final hard-line human advance against the Cylons.

Through this experience, we discover that Gaius is capable of loving someone other than himself, and we also discover that Cylons are capable of psychological trauma that is, in a way, worse than it is for humans, since a Cylon is doomed to retain memories of traumatic experiences when downloading. Trauma is eternal.

In the next episode, Laura is dying and Gaius prepares to step into the presidency. He is reluctant to accept such a large responsibility because he is a weasel. We are once again reminded of his scientific genius. He reports that the fetal blood of the unborn hybrid may be able to cure cancer, a phenomenon he describes as a blessing. His findings include the fact that Cylon blood is virtually indistinguishable from human blood, further erasing the lines of distinction between the two races. The treatment is successful, and Laura is cured.

The next few episodes give the viewer a break from the major story line. We get a glimpse of the underbelly of the fleet in "Black Market," where a number of moral questions are raised. When Lee Adama confronts the leader of the black market, he responds that "it's hard to find the moral high ground when we're all standing in

7. "Pegasus," S2, Ep10, directed by Michael Rymer, written by Anne Cofell Saunders, 0:21:44–0:22:16.

the mud."[8] Lee's character grows increasingly aware of the internal, human battle for justice and morality. We learn that the Cylon Raiders have sentient memory and are resurrected. In "The Captain's Hand," Laura is forced to make a difficult decision regarding women's rights, religious rights, and political freedoms when she is forced to take a stand on the permissibility of abortion. She decides against its legality despite her own personal convictions for the sake of saving the human race. The human population cannot afford to diminish its numbers.

Finally, at the end of the season, we get a flashback that shows the Cylons' perspective. After Caprica Six saves Gaius from the nuclear blast, she downloads into a new body and is celebrated as a hero among the Cylons. She has a new invisible friend, Head Gaius, who appears only to her and is slick and sexy in a pinstripe suit. Ten weeks later, Boomer downloads and awakens in a resurrection "bath." She is also regarded as a hero. Caprica Six is sent to her to help her assimilate. Six opens with a religious appeal, "God loves you."[9] Boomer replies that she does not care. They do not have much in common in their personalities, but one thing binds them together. They have both loved and been loved by a human. This fundamentally changes their view of humanity, and they set out to infiltrate their own kind with a new message. Caprica Six states their mission, "Our people need a new beginning, a way to live in God's love, without hate, without all the lies. All they need is someone to show them the way."[10]

Back on *Galactica*, Sharon goes into labor and surgery is required to help with the baby's delivery. She is named Hera, and is very small, but thriving. In a secret counsel meeting, Laura, Gaius, Adama, and Tigh discuss what should be done with the baby. Laura allows it to live, but only in secret, adopted to a woman in the fleet. Everyone else believes the baby has died, a deception reluctantly

8. "Black Market," S2, Ep14, directed by James Head, written by Mark Verheiden, 0:34:44–0:34:50.

9. "Downloaded," S2, Ep18, directed by Jeff Woolnough, written by Bradley Thompson and David Weddle, 0:14:36–0:14:38.

10. "Downloaded," 0:40:57–0:41:16.

SO SAY WE ALL

arranged for by Doc Cottle. Head Six blames Gaius for failing in his duty to protect the child, "God's will was that our child survive. His will was that she lead the next generation of children. His will was that you protect her."[11]

Emotions are running high on *Galactica* and in the fleet. Tyrol begins to visit a priest for spiritual guidance. The priest is a Cylon called John Cavil. He counsels Tyrol that prayer is useless, "Do you know what [prayer] gets you? Exactly nothing. The gods don't answer prayers. We're here on our own. That's the way they set things up."[12] He also explains that supernatural divinity is an invention by primitive beings who are trying to explain natural phenomena, like the sun setting each night. Cavil's role as a spiritual leader is particularly funny because he is an atheist, or at least he is the Cylon version of a humanist. His beliefs are summed up in one line—"The gods lift up those who lift each other."[13] When another John Cavil appears with the team, they are both arrested. In the brig, the new Cavil explains that Caprica Six and Boomer swayed the way Cylons thought about humans. In response, the Cylons believed themselves to be in error, becoming more like humans, destroying everything in their path. Instead, they should pursue their own path, to become the best machines they can be.

There is a brief respite when Starbuck returns to Caprica to rescue the rebellion led by Anders. Sharon tries to provide helpful intel when questioned, but she is grieving the loss of her baby, once again affirming the Cylon capacity for psychological and emotional trauma.

Political drama unfolds as a presidential election is prepared, naming Laura Roslin and Gaius Baltar as incumbents. With a newly discovered, habitable planet in view, the campaign rests on this issue. Laura believes it is best to press on to find Earth, and Gaius believes it is time to settle. Gaius wins and the human population is resettled on the planet, leaving a skeleton crew to manage

11. "Downloaded," 0:33:40–0:33:54.

12. "Lay Down Your Burdens (Part 1)," S2, Ep19, directed by Michael Rymer, written by Ronald D. Moore, 0:14:00–0:14:06.

13. "Lay Down Your Burdens (Part 1)," 0:33:51–0:33:56.

the fleet of ships in orbit. At the very end of the season, about a year has passed when Cylon ships are detected. The skeleton fleet jumps away and the humans on New Caprica surrender to Cylon occupation.

THEME: SEARCHING FOR THE PROMISED LAND

Like the Israelites in the Hebrew Bible book of Exodus, the remnant of the entire human population has set out from their homes into the wilderness of space. Even the name of their fearless leader, Commander Adama, has a Hebrew heritage. In the Hebrew, *adamah* means "ground" or "earth." You might recognize its famous root word, *adam*, which means "mortal," or" humankind." In *BSG*, Commander Adama bears the weight of humanity. He carefully balances every move to lead the last of humanity to an excellent new settlement and also keep their hopes alive in the process.

When Adama first announced the search for the mythical planet of Earth, he did so to keep hope alive but did not believe in its existence. As the story unfolds, we learn that there are prophecies recorded in the scriptures of Pythia that continually affirm the progress of their journey, especially regarding Laura Roslin as the "dying leader."

The bulk of season two is spent searching for Earth until another prospect is presented, to settle on what becomes New Caprica. The human fleet is exhausted, emotionally weary, and ready to settle. Even though humanity's leaders are still pressing to find Earth, believing it to lead to a better scenario for long-term settlement and repopulation, the people vote to remain. Unfortunately, their respite is short-lived when the Cylons discover the human remnant population. This time, instead of seeking genocide, they seek peace through militarized occupation.

SO SAY WE ALL

CONCLUSION

In the second season, *BSG* introduces characters and stories that press the viewer to judge morality. It becomes increasingly difficult to identify the enemy, primarily when you identify with characters making morally questionable decisions.

Another matter that this season deals with intensively is the emotional and psychological exhaustion felt by the entire human population as they wander around in space trying to bandage needs as they arise, like needing more water, food, and a place to settle. The weariness takes them off track. Instead of pressing onward to find Earth, they settle on a less-than-ideal, yet habitable, planet. Unfortunately, this becomes detrimental when a nuclear blast compromises their location on one of the ships. The occupation of humans by the Cylons confirms they made a horrible decision in voting for Gaius and accepting the least resistant path to settlement.

— 3 —

SEASON 3.0 —
COLLABORATION

SEASON THREE STARTS LIKE an alternate reality of the first season. Instead of destroying the human race, the Cylons occupy New Caprica, bringing "peace" through military control. Cylon Centurions guard the settlement, and some of the human occupants have joined the police force. A small group of humans resist, and they fight like terrorist insurgents. The pool of morality has become filthy, messing with the viewer's sympathies. What are the limits of decency when you become powerless?

There is an emphasis on themes of collaboration and judging the morality of others. This occurs both within the Cylon community and for the humans on New Caprica and after they are rescued and aboard the fleet in space. This comes to climax at the end of the series when Gaius Baltar is placed on trial for treason, and he becomes a scapegoat for every bad thing that happens.

THIRD SEASON CHARACTERS

This season, we get four of the Final Five Cylons. They are revealed at one time at the very end of the season. The shock factor comes into view since these Cylons are not new characters to the show. We have already met them as humans, even early on.

FOUR OF FIVE CYLONS

Colonel Saul Tigh, Tory Foster, Samuel T. Anders, and Chief Galen Tyrol discover they are Cylons simultaneously as the viewer. For the whole episode, the four of them have been listening for a song they can hear playing in the background, coming from within the ship. They seek it out and follow the tune until the four of them simultaneously step into an empty room and realize they have been called here. The song, "All Along the Watchtower" by Bob Dylan, plays loudly, ending the episode.

They are shocked and immediately aware of the irony. The newly revealed Cylons have spent a significant part of their lives fighting against the enemy they now must recognize as themselves. The consequences of the revelation manifest differently for each of them. One thing is clear—things will never be the same on *Galactica*.

HUMAN CHARACTER SPOTLIGHT

Felix Gaeta has been on the series since season one, but he takes on a more complex role this season. He serves in the command center of *Galactica*. In season three, he serves the Gaius Baltar presidency. His insider position provides him with the opportunity to sneak information to the human rebellion, eventually helping them become free from the Cylon occupation.

Cally Henderson Tyrol has been part of the deckhand team since the beginning. Still, her character rises to a place of prominence at the very end of season two, when Chief violently attacks her during a waking nightmare. At the beginning of season three, she is Chief's wife and has a newborn baby. She is a leader in the human rebellion against the Cylons on New Caprica.

SEASON THREE SUMMARY

At the beginning of season three, the Cylons present themselves as forces of order and peaceful rule over the human population on New Caprica. Gaius Baltar is their puppet, the president of the Colonies. His collaboration is one of passive consent. He is fulfilling his duty to the people who elected him by remaining alive and staying in office. He fulfills the expectations of the Cylons by agreeing to collaborate with their efforts, and in exchange, he will not die by their hands—his will to live drives every decision he makes. Eventually, this leads to his signing an executive order that condemns over two hundred humans to death, an action that D'Anna refers to as God's justice. Caprica Six attempts to advocate for him, begging the Cylons not to drag Gaius into their sin. Cavil responds by explaining the necessity of invoking fear for the sake of asserting religious, theocratic order. "If we're bringing the Word of God, then it follows that we should employ any means necessary to do so, any means. Fear is a key article of faith as I understand it, so perhaps it's time to instill a little more fear into the people's hearts and minds."[1] Cavil argues for the Cylons to see the inconsistencies in their actions. They want to achieve peace by means of religious beliefs that encourage violence.

Laura Roslin does what she knows. She is a schoolteacher on New Caprica. However, in her downtime, she keeps a written record of events on New Caprica and reflects on how they will live on this planet with the Cylons. She recalls the time in terms of religious holidays, like "Mars Day," where the god of war is honored. Through her journaling, the viewer learns about her involvement in the insurgency against the Cylon occupation led by Saul Tigh. The human rebellion is an underground terrorist movement. When rations are cut, and the marketplace is banned, human insurgency groups plan suicide bombings and public attacks. Tigh uses religious imagery to describe their position, "We're on the side of the demons, Chief. We're evil men in the gardens of Paradise, sent by the forces of death to spread devastation and destruction wherever we go,"[2] he explains.

1. "Occupation," S3, Ep1, directed by Sergio Mimica-Gezzan, written by Ronald D. Moore, 0:14:55–0:15:10.

2. "Precipice," S3, Ep2, directed by Sergio Mimica-Gezzan, written by Ronald D. Moore, 0:06:42–0:06:55.

Meanwhile, the Cylons are trying to decide how best to create "peace." Their strategy so far has involved killing anyone who counters their leadership. For D'Anna, at least, the quest for peace is religious. She is motivated by pursuing a peaceful existence ordained by the Cylon God. D'Anna is restless and continues to seek guidance for her spiritual journey. Eventually, she finds a human spiritist among the refugees who says she has a message for her. The spiritist encourages D'Anna to pay attention to the spiritual message in her dreams. The prophecy once again obscures the boundaries of faith between the humans and the Cylons. The human spiritual guide tells D'Anna that her fate is somehow tied to the hybrid child named Hera. D'Anna finds a renewed sense of purpose from the oracle and believes that when she is able to find Hera, she will then know what love is. This will surely bring her the peace she seeks.

Following a different strategy, Cavil supports using fear to bring the word of God to the New Capricans. Doral agrees with a violent solution, advocating nuclear genocide. Caprica Six and Boomer oppose his terrorism by defending nonviolent solutions. Leoben takes a more personal approach to proselytization. He kidnaps Starbuck and holds her captive in an apartment. He believes it is the will of God for them to be together based on a spiritual vision.

Occupations such as the one presented in *BSG* happen in our natural world, usually in times of war. Many Westerners have experienced only one side of a conflict: the role of the occupier. *BSG* confronts the Western viewer by presenting a powerless and vulnerable human population under foreign (nonhuman) occupation. The viewer must wrestle with the idea of what it is like to be truly oppressed. Can the Western viewer sympathize with the desperate acts of violence that so many characters advocate? Moreover, both human and Cylon factions justify their actions by appealing to religious ideas and beliefs. The religious motivations force the viewer to consider how views of God and spirituality influence political actions.

The two-part episode entitled "Exodus" describes the eventual freedom of the humans on New Caprica. With the help of the returned *Battlestar Galactica* ship and the *Pegasus*, they fight and win their freedom. The name of the episode refers to the biblical story of the liberation of Hebrew slaves from their Egyptian oppressors, aligning the New Caprican humans with the Israelites of the Bible. The Cylons are the oppressor.

D'Anna enters a personal and spiritual quest to discover the Final Five Cylons. She orders a Centurion to kill her, and in between the moments of death and rebirth, she is in the temple with the Final Five. She explores the knowledge of revelation and the experience of afterlife and concludes that there is something mysterious, ineffable, and miraculous between life and death. D'Anna embarks on a personal spiritual quest to find meaning in life.

The other Cylons discuss the role of the Hybrid, who is a humanoid AI bound to the Baseship. Leoben believes her to be a spiritual figure of some kind, having access to God. When Gaius approaches the Hybrid, she grabs his wrist and speaks to him. The Hybrid talks about the Eye of the Cow. He believes it is a prophecy related to Hera, whose name is affiliated with a mythological Greek goddess who is often represented by a cow. Is this another name for the Eye of Jupiter? D'Anna begins to wonder if there is a connection between the God of the Cylons and the gods of the humans. Through D'Anna's character, the lines between human and Cylon spirituality and existence begin to come together. D'Anna is also instrumental in calling the Final Five out of the fleet in the next season.

Meanwhile, aboard the *Galactica*, Adama, Laura, and Gaeta use Baltar's notes to try and navigate to Earth. They consult the Scrolls of Pythia as well. The scientific and religious texts align in their description of a pulsar star in the head of a lion. When they find the star, an abandoned Cylon ship has been destroyed by a Cylon-specific virus. Athena draws on religious scripture to describe the fallen ship in the wake of an angry God. Aboard the Baseship, they encounter dying Cylons holding hands and reciting a prayer used when facing imminent death without the possibility of downloading. This is as close as the Cylons get to permanent death.

Finding the Cylon-only virus sparks a discussion about the ethics of genocide. Helo adamantly opposes the idea, stating that they would be engaging in the same action they accuse the Cylons of doing. He puts it in religious and moral terms, "I'm talking about right and wrong. I'm talking about losing our souls. Wiping them out with a biological weapon is a crime against humanity." Laura, however, is convinced that humanity must wipe out the mistake of having created the Cylon in the first place. Adama agrees—"So say we all"—affirming a military command with a religious response.[3]

While the characters are trying to sort out their existential crisis, they also have to deal with physical matters, like finding food. Scarcity is a socioeconomic theme raised in "The Passage." Hunger and malnutrition ravage the pilots as they continue to work around the clock in search of food. They eventually find a planet that contains an algae substance suitable to harvest for food. The planet also holds a religious artifact—the Temple of the Five. The Baseship, with Gaius aboard, also arrives at the planet and requests to speak with Adama and negotiate for the possession of this planet. Both Cylons and humans are searching for Earth, and this temple contains the key.

Chief Tyrol has not been very religious up to this point, but the temple awakens something in him. He begins to explore, feeling drawn. Tyrol talks about how much he hated that his dad was a priest. As a kid, he actively tried to defy the gods by committing atrocities in his dad's office. But the temple represents something truly revelatory. He is inspired to work with Laura to find the Eye of Jupiter in the ruins. They believe a marker will point the way to Earth. Tyrol disobeys orders to blast the temple in favor of helping decipher its meaning.

The threat of destroying the temple prompts another debate among the Cylon models. They again disagree on how to deal with the human interference on this planet. D'Anna, the Six, and

---

3. "A Measure of Salvation," S3, Ep7, directed by Bill Eagles, written by Michael Angeli, 0:23:48–0:24:23.

Leoben want to back off to ensure nothing happens to the eye. Cavil chooses the nuclear option, stating that Cylons are machines and will outlive humanity anyway. Meanwhile, D'Anna and Gaius Baltar visit the Hybrid. She tells them that the Final Five will only be revealed to one chosen person. They both want to be that one. They both seek a meaningful existence. D'Anna petitions Caprica Six to pray for her and Gaius as they seek the revelation in the temple.

The Eye of Jupiter, it turns out, is a supernova that miraculously occurs at the exact moment they have all arrived at the temple. The previous nova was four thousand years ago when the Temple was first built. The image of the supernova reminds Helo of paintings created by Starbuck. The viewer is reminded of Leoben's prophecy that Starbuck's destiny was already written. This has all happened before. The gods who went before them were also on a journey. Now, they are on the same path to become like those gods.

During the flash of light, D'Anna sees the Final Five and recognizes them. She asks for their forgiveness before she dies. When she resurrects, a Cavil greets her and informs her she is fundamentally flawed. She disagrees. "It's not a flaw to question our purpose. The one who programmed us, the way we think and why." To which he responds, "Well, that's the problem, right there: the messianic conviction that you're on a special mission to enlighten us."[4] He presses a button, and she shuts down, just like a machine. She is a machine. Meanwhile, during the supernova explosion, Gaius is desperate for a vision and prays earnestly for God to show him the truth. At that moment, Chief knocks him out, and he is returned to *Galactica*.

On *Galactica*, Gaius is imprisoned. Laura and Adama induce him to confess. He describes his experience in religious terms. He tells them that Caprica Six saved him; she "chose me, chose me over all men . . . is she an angel or is she a demon? Is she imaginary,

4. "Rapture," S3, Ep12, directed by Michael Rymer, written by Mark Verheiden, 0:41:33–0:41:50.

or is she real?"[5] He confesses his desire to be a Cylon because it would redeem his sins and provide him with a new beginning of sorts. However, he is not a Cylon, and it is determined that he will undergo a human trial for treason.

As the season moves toward the trial of Gaius Baltar and the revelation of the secret Final Cylon models, individual aspects of humanity are explored in a series of standalone episodes. Many of the themes include ethical and religious facets of everyday life.

Adama deals with the unexpected return of a military comrade who he previously abandoned in "Hero." During this episode, Adama deals with incredible personal guilt and considers resigning his commission. He is not fit to be the leader of the fleet. Laura becomes a voice of reason, awarding him with a medal of distinction. She makes certain he knows that this is for the morale of the crew and to instill hope in the fleet, to give the people a hero.

In "The Woman King," a pandemic sweeps through the refugee camps in the civilian hold of the *Galactica*. We encounter a religious sect called the Sagittaron, a colony with stringent religious views about medicinal treatment. They believe it is a sin against the gods to receive any medicinal treatment. Religious beliefs keep a large mass of the population from accepting treatment or vaccination against a virus that is spreading more rapidly due to the number of people refusing treatment and the necessary close quarters in the refugee camp, a.k.a. "Dogsville." Violent arguments break out when non-Sagittarons realize that exposure to the illness is increased for everyone because of the religious beliefs of a single population. The relevance of this issue cannot be understated in today's world. The episode raises a related ethical matter, forcing a question about whether doctors are under obligation to treat or even help people who believe medicine to be immoral and unethical. At the very least, medical doctors hold to an ethic based on the motto "Do no harm," but Dr. Michael Robert crosses that line in this episode. Believing the ends to justify the means, he murders

5. "Taking a Break from All Your Worries," S3, Ep13, directed by Edward James Olmos, written by Michael Taylor, 0:26:46–0:27:06.

Sagittarons when he has access to them in order to protect the safety of others.

This episode brings to light a very complicated and historic ethical issue when medical science encounters religious beliefs. It is a terrifying story, revealing the potential for extreme cruelty from authority figures who give in to their feelings of prejudice and hatred. It is easy for all authorities to ignore the complaints of a Sagittaron woman in favor of trusting their colleague. But, when Helo forces an investigation, the truth comes out, and Adama and Tigh make it right. They arrest Dr. Robert. But no one wins in the end. The medical staff is already in short supply, and now they have lost a practitioner. The Sagittarons' fears are confirmed. The episode hits hard, and while the story resolves with satisfaction for Helo and Mrs. King, it hits close to home for humanity, especially as we have spent the last two years facing a global pandemic. This prophetic episode is one example of the remarkable ability of sci-fi to engage in ethical and moral matters that examine the very heart of human nature and hold up a mirror, albeit in another galaxy, so that we may see ourselves more clearly. The judgments of other-worldly characters reflect the judgments of ourselves.

The episode "Dirty Hands" raises another ethical matter. When industrial workers begin to sabotage the fuel, they gain the attention of the ship. It is no coincidence that these actions come when Gaius Baltar's Marxist-style propaganda has been circulating. Baltar describes the inequity as a violence inherent in the system. Officers and pilots come from Caprica's well-to-do families, while mechanics and other support workers, who are referred to derogatorily as knuckle-draggers, matriculate from low-income families and regions with fewer resources. The Chief, who led a worker's union on New Caprica, takes a stand and attempts to negotiate with Adama and Laura for a better labor system. The episode recalls the moral and ethical ramifications for a society that encourages people to continue working and living wherever they happen to be when the apocalypse happens. This means that some are lingering on luxury liners while others are engaged in heavy work. Chief's advocacy raises a poignant question: Are we prepared to establish a society where jobs are inherited? This episode draws attention to the kinds of workaday matters that are being dealt with in the fleet regardless of the imminent threats to the existence of humanity. *BSG* raises these stories and encourages us to consider how we should live in the face of imminent danger. This is a theological subject of the ages. The apostle Paul wrote about being faithful in everyday stewardship while simultaneously expecting the coming of the Lord to alter human life as we know it. C. S. Lewis wrote about the importance of faithful living during the looming threats against Britain during WWII. *BSG* offers a similar warning in these episodes, reminding viewers that while the human race is fighting for its very survival, it must also be worthy of survival. This comes by continuing to fight for rights, freedoms, and fundamental worth.

The last episodes of season three lean into the trial of Gaius Baltar and expose significant character developments. Starbuck seeks spiritual guidance from the oracle, who gives her a figurine of the Goddess of the Dawn. The oracle tells her the same as Leoben, that she confused the message with her childhood trauma. Kara was not supposed to lean into her suffering. She was supposed to follow her instincts. Shortly after, her Viper is shot down, and her ship explodes.

Grief is everywhere. Adama, Lee, and Anders grieve the loss of Kara. Saul Tigh mourns his wife, who died on New Caprica. Many are missing friends and family. An emotional storm of loss clouds the crew and fleet as a tribunal is formed to judge Baltar's treason. Five ship captains make up the judicial tribunal. The prosecution is the state. Baltar's defense lawyer, Romo Lampkin, recruits Lee Adama for his team. The players are set.

Meanwhile, Laura, Caprica Six, and Athena continue to share in a vision where Hera is running through the corridors of the Opera House. In the balcony, five shadowy figures look down onto the stage. They represent the Final Five Cylons. During the last two episodes, Tigh, Anders, Tory, and Chief all seem to be hearing music within the ship. They are attuned to the same song. It is a bohemian version of "All Along the Watchtower." The lyrics are scattered throughout the dialogue, and the four characters reflect the emotional confusion, misplaced aggression, and general ennui. They are revealed at the very end, after following the music to an empty corridor and arriving simultaneously, to be aware that they are Cylons—four of the Final Five.

While Baltar is imprisoned, he gains recognition as a spiritual leader. A woman comes to him asking for his blessing over her sick child. He responds, "I'm terribly sorry. I can't help you. I'm not god, the God, or god of any derivation thereof." Several have come to him in this fashion, and many more have written letters. Head Six believes this is his fate, "I saw a woman in pain, a woman who can see you more clearly than you can see yourself."[6] Like Laura Roslin, imprisonment exalted his status to spiritual leader.

In the tribunal, the accusation against Baltar is the loss of five thousand souls during his presidency on New Caprica. The trial proceeds, and it is emotional and raw. Laura testifies to the execution. Lee, now acting as an entirely civilian member of Baltar's defense, accuses her of taking a drug known for inducing hallucinations, the Kamala extract. Then, Saul Tigh is called to the stand and is drunk. He ends up confessing that he murdered his wife, Ellen, for treason. In the background, Adama states that he has no intention of letting Gaius be pardoned, no matter what evidence is brought. It soon becomes plain to the viewer that whatever Gaius's crimes, there is little reason to charge him alone with treason when so many people have behaved so badly. Lee Adama makes a final appeal to justice for the sake of humanity and integrity. His speech hinges on the nature of forgiveness. For all the pardons and forgiveness for unbelievable individual crimes against humanity, Gaius is being asked to take upon himself the burden of unforgiveness. The question of the necessity of a being to take on the responsibility of all human sin is a sizeable theological problem, the extent of which could not be covered here. The thing that seems clear in Lee's speech is that for all the forgiveness there appears to be a demand that one at least pays the penalty of guilt on behalf

6. "Crossroads, Part 1," S3, Ep19, directed by Michael Rymer, written by Michael Taylor, 0:05:38–0:05:44.

of the many. Can Gaius bear that responsibility? Should Gaius be the one to assume that responsibility? Would it even matter to the remnant of humanity?

"We make our own laws now, our own justice," Lee says, "and we've been pretty creative in letting people off the hook. We're on the run. We have to fight to survive. We have to improvise. But, not this time, no, not this time, not for Gaius Baltar. You," Lee says as he points to the defendant, "you have to die. You have to die because, well, we don't like you very much. And we, the mob, we want to throw you out the airlock. That's justice." Lee goes on to describe the scapegoating of Gaius Baltar in his final words. "This is about anger, vengeance, and mostly about shame. About the guilt of those of us who ran away. We are trying to dump all that guilt and all that shame and then flush him out of the airlock and hope that he gets rid of it all so we can live with ourselves. But that won't work. That won't work because that's not justice."[7]

Lee's appeal to justice and humanity's need for a scapegoat (or a messiah) to bear the responsibility of all the collective shame and guilt for the sake of justice works. Gaius is acquitted, and when met with hostility, he is rescued by women who cloak him and take him to safety.

This whole courtroom scene is a messianic play. Gaius is tried for crimes against humanity, even as we discover that there are as many crimes to go around as there are people. However, he is not crucified, as Christ was, but his life remains under threat. He is, as the Christ, met by women who tend to the care and safety of his body (and more!). It is not a perfect metaphor, but the Christo-centric imagery is there in Gaius Baltar. He is a scapegoat. He is a messiah. He is human. In season three, Gaius Baltar's character aligns with religious views of Western Abrahamic faith traditions. His transformation into a spiritual leader evolves and increases in the final season.

7. "Crossroads, Part 2," S3, Ep20, directed by Michael Rymer, written by Mark Verheiden, 0:23:25–0:25:39.

THEME: COLLABORATION

Collaboration is a season three theme. Humans collaborate with the Cylon leaders to suppress violence in the occupation of New Caprica. Sharon, a Cylon, collaborates with Adama, becoming his chief confidant aboard the *Galactica*. Once the New Capricans return to the space fleet, a committee hunts down human collaborators and sentences them to death. At the end of the season, Gaius is put on trial for treason. He has committed the ultimate act of collaboration by surrendering to the Cylons.

This idea of earning or betraying trust, depending on which side the story gives us, is a significant consequence of collaboration. The humans who collaborate with Cylons wear masks to hide their faces so their fellow humans will not harm them. They feel justified in their actions because it is for the sake of peace. However, they commit violent atrocities. When a secret committee explores the nuances of their services on the *Galactica*, the issues become less clear. What of those who signed on with the Cylon contingent to gain a bit of power that allows them to help their own? Jammer, for one, complicates matters when he claims to have set Cally free during the massacre attempt on New Caprica. Can one human judge the morality of another?

Season three picks up several months after the Cylon occupation, and in that time, Sharon has become a close confidant and friend to Admiral Adama aboard the *Galactica*. It becomes clear that she has earned his trust when he (re)instates her to the total rank previously held by Boomer. This seems a little bit odd because she is not Boomer, and at the same time perfectly reasonable because she has Boomer's memories. Once again, we are faced with personhood—is a person more than the sum of their memories? In this case, Sharon is and is not Boomer. There is wisdom in keeping her close since she can betray Adama's trust. But, Adama is not playing a game of strategy here as much as he is acting out forgiveness. He wants to forgive her. She is family, after all, and she has proved her worth many times over. This is a far cry from a season ago when she plugs into the *Galactica* to save them all, and Adama orders her taken back to the prison cell, diminishing her person-hood with his order: "Take this *thing* back to its cell."[8] Adama and Sharon are civilized. They drink coffee together and speak about philosophy and the power of forgiveness and trust in their rela-tionship. The civility between them camouflages the hypocrisy of the collaboration. Eventually, Sharon is also (mostly) accepted by the crew. She is granted a new call sign, "Athena," named for the goddess of wisdom and warfare.

Meanwhile, for most of the series, Gaius Baltar is aboard a Cylon vessel. Even though he surrendered to the Cylons and did everything they asked, his life under constant threat, he was nei-ther trusted nor accepted by the Cylons. He would be a prisoner wherever he was. Only Caprica Six had feelings for him that kept him alive. He was her pet. His collaboration was not voluntary, but at least he was safe from the humans aboard the Cylon Basestar.

Collaboration shifts the perspective a little. The boundary increasingly blurring between Cylon and human is now wholly shuffled. There are humans with the Cylons and Cylons with the humans, and the Cylons have divided among themselves into ma-jor factions with different minds about their purpose. They have become more like the humans in their discord.

The end of the season puts the spotlight again on collabora-tion during Gaius Baltar's trial. Justice, in its simplest form, wishes to deny anyone their efforts of collaboration and put the onus of the burden of guilt on one man, a scapegoat, instead. Gaius Baltar, the elected leader of the Colonies, is tried for the loss of human lives.

The idea that anyone could be held responsible for the actions of a homicidal enemy is difficult to justify, yet humanity reaches for this repeatedly. Just in the last century, we have looked for someone to blame for the devastation of 9/11, and in the pres-ent decade, for someone to blame for the number of human lives lost due to ineptitude and the inability to stop the COVID-19 pandemic. The question of whether or not we can hold one per-son responsible for the complex events that lead up to and cause

8. "Flight of the Phoenix," 0:35:24–0:35:27.

destruction is an ancient one. The biblical book of Leviticus gives us a picture of an antique set of rules and guidelines that attempt to create systems of justifications and payments for wrongdoings. The ones that cannot be paid because the price is too high are set upon the shoulders of an animal, a beast of burden, the scapegoat. In the *BSG* trial, the people petition for Baltar to become that beast, just as on New Caprica the Cylons also forced him to sign an executive order for mass execution so that he would truly be their scapegoat, relinquishing their guilt as well. Even though the trial grants him amnesty, Gaius is the one upon whom all blame is laid. This sets the stage for his next role as a religious figurehead, a *messiah*, heralding the shape of things to come for both Cylons and humans together. Baltar's transformation is not merely a sign of political and social collaboration with the Cylons; it is also a sign of religious collaboration, or conversion, to the Cylon God.

CONCLUSION

The third season of *BSG* explores many ethical issues, including collaboration with the enemy, religious freedoms, terrorism, career election, genocide, interspecies marriage, child-centered family units, and more. At the beginning of this season, humanity has just settled on a new planet, along with all their hopes and dreams of a permanent future. The Cylons suddenly arrive and occupy the planet, acting as dictators through their mouthpiece, Gaius Baltar. The season deals with how and why humanity deserves to survive and asks questions about the fundamental differences between the Cylons and the humans. In the end, we discover that not only are the Cylons more like the humans than seemed possible even a season ago, but key human characters are revealed to have been Cylons all along. By the end of this season, the question about who deserves to live extends beyond a simplistic "Us-versus-Them" model that prefers humanity. Some Cylons share virtues with humans, and some humans act like the enemy. *BSG* breaks down presumptions about who should win in the end. The series uses religious views to distinguish between the Cylons who believe in one true God and the pantheistic humans. Religious views shift among humans who begin to believe in the virtue of the Cylon God. As religious beliefs shift, so go the political and social thoughts and attitudes of the characters. Religion walks hand in hand with social evolution.

— 4 —

SEASON 4.0 —
EXISTENTIAL CRISIS
& ENLIGHTENMENT

THE FINAL SEASON OF *BSG* deals with resolution between characters. Humans and Cylons are pressed to deal with their identity and what that means for the alliances they make.

Now that four of the Final Five Cylons are revealed to be humans, most of whom have been leaders in the fight against the Cylons from the very beginning, the "Us-versus-Them" discussion gets really cluttered. The season reaches a climax when they find Earth, and it is an unlivable wasteland. Piecing together disjointed memories from their past, the final Cylons can remember some of what happened. At least they can find some solace in their importance. The next big turning point occurs when *Galactica* is physically breaking down. The tentative alliance between Cylons and humans becomes solidified when the Cylons offer Cylon technology to repair the *Galactica* in exchange for alliance. Many from both races see this as a betrayal of their heritage. But it is more a sign of the strengthening of bonds between the two races.

The human side of the Cylon is on display with Caprica Six's pregnancy with Col. Tigh. They even talk about the hope of the Cylon race continuing without the help of humans. But this is quickly dispelled when she has a miscarriage. Hera, the Cylon human hybrid child, is their genuine hope for an integrated future. Both races can live peacefully, together, in a new homeworld, but they must share their children to build a bridge of peace.

It is a kind of mirror to what Laura and Adama realized in the miniseries—if we are going to survive, we need to start making babies. In the end, mere survival wasn't enough. It wasn't going to build a peaceful tomorrow. But, human procreation with Cylons will become the key to ending the fight. Peace would be achieved through shared family.

FOURTH SEASON CHARACTERS

There are no explicitly new characters in this final season. However, the last of the Final Five Cylons is revealed, and a human character returns from the dead. A few characters who have already played significant roles in the series take on a more intense and altered version of themselves.

FINAL CYLON REVELATIONS

The last Cylon of the Final Five is revealed to be a woman we already met—Ellen Tigh. She is reborn on a Baseship and met by John Cavil. She seems to have almost an entirely different personality. She is composed and professional, even-tempered, and she remembers everything. Unlike the other Final Five, she is not "turned on" in her human status. Ellen can fill in the gaps of the Cylon story and reveal answers to many questions.

We learn about the never entirely revealed Model Seven, called Daniel. This is a significant mystery since Kara Thrace's estranged father is named Daniel. This is not revisited in the series but leaves some space for future exploration of the *BSG* canon.

SHIFTING HUMAN CHARACTERIZATION

Kara Thrace returns from the dead, and she is what Gaius Baltar refers to as an "angel." Her demeanor is entirely altered for most of the season. She is almost always buttoned up in a neatly pressed uniform, her hair smoothly tied back. She still has moments of outburst, and for a short time, while trying to trace a faint memory of Earth, she goes Captain Ahab-style crazy. By the end of the season, she comes to terms with her postdeath existence.

SEASON FOUR SUMMARY

Season four opens with the recently acquitted Gaius Baltar. The first episode is entitled "He That Believeth in Me," referencing a verse in the New Testament—"Jesus said unto her, I am the resurrection, and the life: he that believeth in me, though he were dead, yet shall he live: and whosoever liveth and believeth in me shall never die. Believest thou this?" (John 11:25–26 KJV). The titular reference to this biblical passage frames the messianic characterization of Gaius Baltar for the final season. Immediately after his trial, a group of women takes him into their care. Baltar is indignant and ungrateful. He calls himself a king of fools, and he refers to his groupies as a looney bin, especially when he sees the shrine featuring a photo of him surrounded by light. He is unable to die and reluctant to lead. He is on a journey to realize his fate as a spiritual leader.

Head Six tells Gaius that this is his destiny. He must preach about the one true God. Shortly after arriving, he is called upon to pray for a little boy whose mother believes him to be close to death. Gaius prays to the one God, the God of the Cylons, rather than the human gods his followers expect him to pray to. He offers his life in exchange for the boy's health, pleading, "Please God, I'm asking you this one last time. Don't let this child die. Has he sinned against you? He can't have sinned against you. He's not even had a life yet. How can you take him and let me live? After all I've done."[1] Gaius seems sincerely repentant, confessing his unworthiness. Shortly after this, he is attacked by civilians, and he offers himself to them, expecting to die. His keepers step in, and Gaius lives. Upon his return to the shared quarters, he finds the boy has recovered from his illness. Head Six explains that he has a higher calling. Gaius Baltar moves from his acquittal as the scapegoat for all the sins of the fleet at the end of season three to becoming a reluctant spiritual leader, an evangelist for the Cylon God.

Laura, on the other hand, begins to fade as her cancer treatments intensify in this season. While she is in treatment, she meets another woman who is dying from cancer. Emily has found comfort in the teachings of Gaius that are broadcast via radio. She tells Laura about her vision of the afterlife, a river crossed by ferry toward departed loved ones. She speaks about "this presence, hovering all around me, warm, loving, and it said, 'Don't be scared, Emily. I am with you. Hold my hand, and we'll cross over together.'"[2] Laura is skeptical, arguing that Baltar preaches about the Cylon God. Emily says a true God is God of all; she makes fun of the Lords of Kobol. Laura tries to explain they are metaphors. Shortly afterward, Emily seizes up, and Laura is on a boat with Emily looking at a group of happy people on the river's shore. Emily is with them. Then, the scene changes, and Laura's family is standing on the beach. She whispers that she's not ready. When she wakes up, she hears Gaius Baltar's broadcast streaming. He talks about God leading you to the other side of the river. The afterlife Emily experienced is somehow connected with the Cylon God.

The newly formed faction of four of the Final Five Cylons tries to work out who the fifth Cylon might be. Chief believes Baltar's newfound religion means he can help. He refers to Baltar's

1. "He That Believeth in Me," S4, Ep1, directed by Michael Rymer, written by Bradley Thompson and David Weddle, 0:33:10–0:33:43.

2. "Faith," S4, Ep6, directed by Michael Nankin, written by Seamus Kevin Fahey, 0:25:50–0:26:12.

group as "One-God Nutcases."[3] When Tory interviews Gaius, he describes his calling in terms of music, a metaphor that has its roots in the previous season when the four Cylons discover their own identities. Gaius says, "It seems that God has chosen me to sing his song . . . a grotesque screeching cacophony becomes a single melody."[4] Over several episodes, their conversations about religion and the gods reveal their different perspectives about the divine. After his wife dies, Tyrol visits Gaius and finds some peace and a way toward redemption.

Religious tensions heighten when a terrorist group called The Sons of Aries begins making trouble on the ship. They believe they represent "the old gods." Head Six warns Gaius, "The old gods are fighting back."[5] He feels threatened and challenged, pressing him to speak out more boldly. He destroys a temple, throwing down their idols and speaking out against what he calls faceless gods. Laura and the political quorum discuss the protection of Baltar's group and precedents for religious discrimination in a changing world. After Baltar survives a beating, with the help of Head Six, who is his guardian angel at this point, he strengthens his position. He confesses his selfishness and speaks about a God who sparked life and dwells in every person. His message sounds like a mix of humanism and various religious ideas, including Hinduism and the divine spark, Buddhism and the pursuit of enlightenment, and Abrahamic faiths with a supreme creator. He stands before a large crowd, his body bloodied and his clothes torn, telling them, "The truth is we are perfect just as we are. God only loves that which is perfect, and he loves you because you are perfect. You are perfect just as you are."[6] This is the beginning of Gaius, the religious leader. Throughout the rest of the season, Gaius speaks about prayer,

---

3. "Six of One," S4, Ep2, directed by Anthony Hemingway, written by Michael Angeli, 0:12:14–0:12:15.

4. "Six of One," 0:22:12–0:22:45.

5. "Escape Velocity," S4, Ep4, directed by Edward James Olmos, written by Jane Espenson, 0:14:57–0:14:59.

6. "Escape Velocity," 0:42:35–0:42:56.

SO SAY WE ALL

accepting truth, and love from God. He advocates belief in one God over the gods humans have tried to serve.

Meanwhile, another resurrection is about to happen when Kara Thrace reappears in a sparkling, brand-new-looking Viper. Her return is a miracle, but Adama doesn't believe in miracles and he joins Lee in watching the replay of Kara's initial explosion. They cannot believe she survived. Adama is cynical, but he concludes that her return is a true miracle. Starbuck is in the brig, but she claims to know the way to Earth. She insists they are going the wrong way due to an internal and inexplicable sensation that Earth is calling to her. The prodigal Starbuck possesses an ethereal spirituality that she claims will lead them all to Earth, and to their salvation.

On the Cylon Baseship, the Cylons argue about the religious nature of the Hybrid's ramblings. Is it nonsense or prophecy? The Cylons take sides against each other based on their religious beliefs. The Sixes, Eights, and Twos (Leoben) believe the Hybrid speaks a prophetic truth and that the Final Five are in the human fleet. John Cavil (One) disagrees, and the Fours and Fives join him, along with Boomer, who votes against her model. They believe any discussion of the Final Five is forbidden. Cavil believes machines are machines and nothing else—logistics and science, without religion and the humanities. He says, "Look, millions of Twos have that nose, Sixes that mouth, Eights those breasts, Ones have this brain; we're mechanized copies."[7] The Sixes and their faction believe that Centurions and Raiders deserve the right to free will and autonomy. Cavil wants to lobotomize Raiders who refuse orders. The Sixes argue that lobotomizing them is against God's divine will. Cavil argues for the machineness of them all, while the others argue for the pursuit of a divine purpose. The division between Cylons leads to conflict that centers on finding the Final Five Cylons. The Sixes negotiate to unbox D'Anna (Three) and reveal the identities of the Five.

Back on *Galactica*, Admiral Adama gives Kara Thrace a small ship and crew to try and find her way back to Earth. She also uses music as a metaphor, describing her search as looking for a "tune"

7. "Six of One," 0:09:44–0:09:53.

to reunite her thoughts. They come across a Leoben Cylon who speaks in terms of faith and religion, telling her, "God has taken your hand."[8] He explains the Cylon civil war and asks for an alliance. He tells Kara she is an "angel blazing with the light of God."[9] He speaks of the revelation of God's plan, and they discover a map to a Cylon Baseship that has been attacked. Aboard the Baseship, Kara meets the Cylon Hybrid connected to the ship. The Hybrid looks directly at her and quotes the human scripture of Pythia, "Thus will it come to pass—a dying leader will know the truth of the Opera House," then adds, "The missing Three will give you the Five, who have come from the home of the Thirteenth. You are the harbinger of death, Kara Thrace; you will lead them all to their end. End of line."[10] They take the Baseship to the fleet to request an alliance for the sake of finding the Final Five and discovering the way to Earth. Starbuck questions her existence—is she savior or destroyer? Her personal quest for meaning continues to haunt her, but it does not keep her from staying the course to fulfill her promise to Adama.

The humans work with the Cylons to unbox D'Anna, and in the process, they destroy the Resurrection Ship. Natalie Faust, the Six who negotiates with the humans, says they believe their lives don't have meaning without death, without mortality. She refers to mortality as a flaw that humans spend their lives trying to overcome, but without it, there is no meaning to life. When the Resurrection Hub is destroyed after D'Anna is unboxed, an Eight comments that trust will be more easily built now that Cylons and humans are both mortals. Mortality as meaning is a trope often recalled in sci-fi and fantasy literature. Whereas many religions seek eternal existence in an afterlife, literary immortals seek the solace and comfort of death. The temporary nature of life is what makes relationships so meaningful.

8. "The Road Less Traveled," S4, Ep5, directed by Michael Rymer, written by Mark Verheiden, 0:12:24–0:12:25.

9. "The Road Less Traveled," 0:33:29–0:33:31.

10. "Faith," 0:29:52–0:30:17.

Laura, Caprica Six, and Athena continue to have a vision of Hera running through the Opera House. A simulation of the vision takes place when Hera runs through the corridors on *Galactica*. Athena and Laura cross each other in the hallway, and Natalie sees Hera and talks to her, lifting her to hold her. Athena takes Hera and then shoots and kills Natalie out of fear. As Natalie lies dying in the medical bay, she has a vision of the same river-crossing previously seen by Laura and Emily. We realize that the Cylon and human afterlife is one and the same.

Meanwhile, Laura seeks out the Hybrid on the Baseship to finally discover the meaning behind the Opera House. She is among those who believe the Hybrid has special knowledge. She takes Gaius with her, and the ship unexpectedly jumps away. Meanwhile, Laura experiences a series of visions while the Baseship jumps through space. She sees Elosha, her spiritual guide who died on Kobol. Elosha wants to teach her a lesson about accepting love from people close to her. Laura realizes that *Galactica* has become her home.

While they are on the Baseship, Gaius begins a missional conversation with a Centurion Cylon. He tells the Centurion about God, saying, "He's your God as well, and God does not want any of his creation to be slaves."[11] Gaius tells a parable about a dog waiting for its master's permission to eat. His use of legends to preach about freedom for all God's people likens him to Jesus, the Christ in the New Testament, who used parables to explain relationships between individuals and God. His transformation from sacrificial scapegoat to messiah is nearly complete.

Gaius Baltar becomes severely injured in an explosion after his conversation with the Centurion, and Laura is the only one nearby to treat his wounds. He lies on a bench with his arms out, bleeding from his side. He is the image of the crucifixion. Laura considers allowing him to bleed to death, while Gaius speaks of love. "You need God, Laura,"[12] he says. He talks about how God

11. "Hub," S4, Ep9, directed by Paul Edwards, written by Jane Espenson, 0:23:26–0:23:33.

12. "Hub," 0:28:12–0:28:16.

took away his pain, his "soul-breaking guilt,"[13] and transformed him. The message is very similar to the Christian message of conversion and salvation. Being healed and transformed because of God's goodness is reminiscent of the writings by the apostle Paul in the New Testament. Laura fights her urge to kill him, and once again Gaius Baltar is saved from death. They are all saved when the Baseship finally reunites with *Galactica*.

The four Cylons on the fleet are stressed and still wary of the allied Cylons. When D'Anna shows up on *Galactica*, she invites the four Cylons in the fleet to join her on the Baseship, and Tory goes. Anders, Chief, and Tigh hear music that draws them to the Viper that returned with Kara. The Viper's console displays a signal from Earth. Their identities are no longer a secret; Adama is distraught. He questions the purpose of everything they have done, only to eventually learn that Cylons are among their own fleet, even among those he calls family.

Adama makes the final decision that the entire fleet will follow the coordinates on the signal. Adama appeals to the fleet to move quickly and in unity. It is the last push. When they arrive, Earth is destroyed, a wasteland, and the Final Four Cylons begin to remember where they came from. Saul Tigh realizes that Ellen was the fifth Cylon. Furthermore, they confirm that the thirteenth tribe was made up of Cylons.

The realization that humans and Cylons have more in common than not is complicated for several characters to comprehend. Laura begins to question every religious ideology she embraced along the way. She sets to burning the scriptures of Pythia, page by page. She resigns her responsibilities as president, and she leaves the presidency as well, saying, "I've played my role in this farce. 'The dying leader will guide the people to blah blah blah frakin' blah blah.'"[14] Lee Adama, who has become the civilian leader, makes a speech that sets aside religion, stating that they are no longer bound to the ramblings of Pythia and can continue on their

13. "Hub," 0:28:39–0:28:41.

14. "A Disquiet Follows My Soul," S4, Ep12, directed by Ronald D. Moore, written by Ronald D. Moore, 0:27:17–0:27:29.

SO SAY WE ALL

path. Eventually, Admiral Adama seeks comfort from his oldest friend, Saul Tigh, who was only recently identified as a Cylon.

On Earth, Kara and Leoben follow a signal to a burnt Viper with skeletal remains in it. She recognizes her Viper and finds her military tags and wedding ring on the body. The ones she wears are identical. Kara spends the rest of the season trying to reconcile who or what she is until Gaius announces she is an angel walking among her loved ones, a sign that there is life after death.

Ellen's story is revealed as a flashback, where she awakens in a Cylon bath. John Cavil is present. They talk and fill in the story of their past and Cavil's resentment toward his "parents"—the Final Five. He refers to Ellen as his creator, saying the Final Five trapped him in this body because they felt it was destined by God. Cavil sees himself as a victim. Ellen, Cavil, and Boomer discuss what it means to be a machine versus being human.

As Ellen's story is told, we discover that Anders has taken a bullet in the brain. This prompted his memory of the past, and he describes how the Final Five invented resurrection and tried to warn the humans to treat AI well and avoid conflict. He reveals the existence of a Model Seven called Daniel (who Kara believes to be her father). He speaks of angels and warns the Cylons to remain with the fleet and work with the humans. He does not regain consciousness after the surgery.

When Boomer helps Ellen escape and return to the *Galactica*, the Final Five argue about remaining with the fleet or going their separate ways. Tigh reaches an emotional breaking point and makes a speech about how the *Galactica* is his home. His family is with the fleet. He blames Ellen for causing friction that resulted in Caprica Six falling ill and losing their baby. Tigh is tormented by grief and talks about how they must have invented a compassionate God for their Cylon creation to believe in since the five of them are not unified. He turns to Adama for comfort while mourning the loss of his baby.

Conflicts between humans and Cylons become more personal after Adama approves Cylon technology to save the *Galactica*, keeping the ship intact. Felix Gaeta becomes particularly irritable and joins with Zarek to mount a political coup. Baltar appeals to Gaeta, telling him if he is looking for redemption this will not work. He and Laura are sent off the *Galactica*, and in one of my favorite scenes, Admiral Adama and Saul Tigh turn to fight for the return of the *Galactica*. In the end, Gaeta and Zarek are unsuccessful, and they are both executed for the insurrection. The fate of Galactica is now sealed—Cylons and humans are allied for better or worse. They will forge the future together.

Elsewhere, Kara Thrace faces a personal existential crisis. While she is in the bar drinking, she begins to chide a piano player. They develop a friendship. He reminds her of her dad, who left her when she was young. The piano man is writing a song that sounds familiar to her. The child Hera gives Kara a drawing of twelve colorful stars, but she realizes that when turned sideways, it is a musical construction. The piano man plays the notes, and it is the tune that switched on the Final Five. Kara also recognizes the music. Tigh and Ellen are in the bar when Kara plays the song, and they realize that Hera is somehow part of an overarching story that binds them all together. Shortly afterward, the man disappears, and it turns out no one has ever seen him. Kara's experience was singular and supernatural. The piano man was her angel, a conversation partner to help her work out the mystery of the song, its purpose, and her path.

In another part of the ship, Chief Tyrol and Boomer reconnect while she is in the brig. He lets her out, and she kidnaps Hera, "the shape of things to come." Kara appeals to Adama that Hera may be humanity's only hope. She recognizes the significance of her drawing out the music that is connected to the Cylons and herself. Adama responds in anger that it must be destiny that drives them. He's finished with destiny, and with that renounces his belief in prophecy and gods in all forms. However, he cannot bring himself to fight against his crew and he decides to send a small rescue party.

Meanwhile, Gaius Baltar is speaking more and more about angels present in the fleet, whose existence proves life after death. He says, "I don't believe that Angels appear to you in some mystical spectral form. Angels take the guise of those nearest and dearest to you. Those who understand your doubts and your trials and can steer you back to the road of salvation. I believe in Angels because I see them."[15] When Kara finds him, she tells him she is dead and shows him two sets of her tags and her wedding ring. She gives him the set found on the body and tells him to run some tests. "There's one thing I know for sure," she says, "I'm not an Angel."[16] She sits with Anders, who is in a Cylon bath, hooked up to machinery that keeps him alive. He is connected to *Galactica* in several ways. When she plugs him in, he grabs her arm and looks at her in the face, repeating the Baseship Hybrid's earlier words, "You are the harbinger of death, Kara Thrace."[17] When they realize he has become like the Cylon Hybrid, capable of controlling the ship, he is unplugged.

The final scene before the series ends is a mass funeral for all the lives, Cylon and human, that were lost when the ship became unstable in one of the areas being repaired. Three memorial services are held simultaneously. Adama leads a service for the humans, Ellen for the Cylons, and Gaius holds a memorial. In a montage sequence, each memorial shows a similar sentiment being performed in a different manner.

Admiral Adama leads the humans in a military service. He appeals to the duty and honor of those who died, saying, "We must understand that what we sacrifice here today are women and men of extreme courage." The crowd chants together at the end, "So say we all. So say we all. So say we all."[18]

Gaius leads his followers in a service of comfort, saying, "And so we mourn the passing of our friends because that is what we are, voyagers traversing the stars in search of grace, unity, life, love."[19]

15. "Islanded in a Stream of Stars," S4, Ep18, directed by Edward James Olmos, written by Michael Taylor, 0:11:02–0:11:32.

16. "Islanded in a Stream of Stars," 0:20:30–0:20:32.

17. "Islanded in a Stream of Stars," 0:23:19–0:23:20.

18. "Islanded in a Stream of Stars," 0:31:40–0:32:20.

19. "Islanded in a Stream of Stars," 0:31:40–0:32:20.

Ellen touches sacred water to her head and leads the Cylons with her in prayer to God, "We must remember there is a higher purpose. Heavenly Father, grant us the strength, the wisdom, and above all, a measure of acceptance however small." Together at the end, the small crowd says in unison, "Grace, unity, life, love."[20]

The conglomerate funerary scene not only reveals the beginning of racial and cultural inclusion, but also demonstrates a religiously diverse community. It is remarkably different from the first funeral ceremony which takes place at the end of the *BSG Miniseries*. As *BSG* moves toward its finale, we experience a stronger sense of inclusion in the fleet, accompanied by a sense of relief, even peace. After the ceremonies, Gaius Baltar commands the attention of the room, speaking about life after death, "the gift of eternal life that is offered to every one of us." He appeals to a sense of courage upon embracing death that allows anyone to "cross over"[21] into eternal life. He names Starbuck alone, who has done just that. He has proven scientifically, by testing the blood on the tags she found earlier on a corpse, that Kara Thrace has died. After this, Kara reconciles herself to what has happened and places her own picture on the memorial wall of those who died.

SERIES FINALE SUMMARY

The series finale is a three-part episode that includes flashback story arcs to tell some of the backstories of prominent characters. The audience gains a little more understanding about how these people ended up in service on the *Galactica*. These stories tell of significant personal loss, heartache, compromise, and denial. Wherever the journey began, they all ended up in the same place, guiding humans through their final journey to Earth.

Twelve notes of music become central to the plot of "Daybreak." Kara Thrace feels her task is to decipher a code, "Hera wrote the notes to a song that my father used to play for me, the

---

20. "Islanded in a Stream of Stars," 0:31:40–0:32:20.
21. "Islanded in a Stream of Stars," 0:32:59–0:33:08.

same song that led us to Earth."[22] And it was, coincidentally (or maybe not!), the same song that switched the Final Five Cylons on. Anders has become a conduit for the *Galactica* in the same way the Cylon Hybrids are for the Cylon Baseships. In a flashback, he speaks about his love for perfection. His commitment to Pyramid is his search for "the perfect throw, the perfect catch . . . those moments when you can feel the perfection of creation, the beauty of physics, the wonder of mathematics, the relation of action and reaction."[23] Kara seeks the perfect union of music and mathematics, assigning numbers as values to the twelve notes of her song.

Admiral Adama is persuaded to take a more active role when he finds a photo of Hera and decides to run a volunteer-only rescue mission. In one of the most heartwarming scenes in the series, Adama gives a speech to rally one last mission to rescue Hera from Cavil and the Cylons. He tapes a line to the floor, and he asks volunteers to step on one side of the line. Anders and his Cylon bath are plugged into the central command to guide the ship and communicate with the Cylon ships. It is a complete integration of the human and Cylon technologies on the *Galactica*. The volunteer crew is made up of Cylons, Centurions, and humans. They are all united by a common enemy.

Toward the end of Hera's rescue, Laura sees the Opera House vision with Hera and looks for her. Helo is shot from behind, and while Athena is helping him, Hera runs away, frightened. Athena chases her and flashes to the vision of the Opera House. Hera runs past all the guns. Laura walks through corridors, looking for her. Cavil also comes, with several Centurions. Laura sees Hera and holds her, hiding her from Cavil and his army. She runs off again. Laura and Athena see each other across the corridor and run in the same direction. They see Hera. She walks right up to Gaius and Caprica Six, who take her to safety behind a closed door. Gaius can see the Opera House, and as they enter the Opera House, they are

22. "Daybreak, Part 1," S4, Ep19, directed by Michael Rymer, written by Ronald D. Moore, 0:00:40–0:00:48.

23. "Daybreak, Part 1," S4, Ep19, directed by Michael Rymer, written by Ronald D. Moore, 0:27:58–0:28:32.

actually standing in *Galactica's* Combat Information Center (CIC). Several are dead. Adama shoots a Cylon and kicks the corpse. The Final Five are standing above, lit from behind, just like the earlier vision which haunted their dreams during the series. This is fate.

Cavil takes a more aggressive stance. He wants Hera, believing her to be the key to the Cylons' survival. Gaius responds with a speech about her importance to humanity as well. He talks about prophecy and all the unexplainable things that have happened to lead them all to this point. "There is another force at work here." He goes on to speak about the unusual dreams and loved ones who have died and returned to them, "whether we want to call that God, or gods, or some sublime inspiration, or a divine form that we can't know or understand, it doesn't matter. It's here. It exists, and our two destinies are entwined in its force."[24]

Cavil asks how he can know God is on his side, and Gaius responds, "God's not on anyone's side. God's a force of nature, beyond good and evil. Good and evil—we created those. Want to break the cycle? That's in our hands and our hands only. It requires a leap of faith."[25] In Gaius Baltar's final speech, we get a description of the theology of unity. There is one supreme being capable of uniting everyone by different means of religious expressions. They are all connected through God. Differences between Cylons and humans, Centurions and hybrids are irrelevant to the gift of grace and access to resurrection.

The *Galactica* must execute one last jump away from the exploding Cylon ships. Kara inputs the numbers she has assigned to her song, and the *Galactica* arrives in orbit of a planet that resembles our real-world Earth. They scout the continent of Africa and find tribal people. To start again and give humanity a second chance, they decide to spread out and live off the land, abandoning their technology. Lee Adama describes this in spiritual terms. "Our brains have always outweighed our hearts," he says. "Our

---

24. "Daybreak, Part 2," S4, Ep20, directed by Michael Rymer, written by Ronald D. Moore, 0:39:55–0:40:41.

25. "Daybreak, Part 2," 0:41:00–0:41:35.

science charges ahead; our souls lag behind. Let's start anew."[26] On New Earth, many part ways, walking separate paths, spreading out across the globe.

The very ending of the series is a flash-forward to "Modern-Day Planet Earth," 150,000 years later. Head Six and Head Gaius walk through a crowded city and talk about the cyclical nature of humanity. They speak about God's plan as the Jimi Hendrix version of "All Along the Watchtower" plays us out.

THEME: SURRENDER

A critical theological theme in season four is surrender. The entire series has built up to several moments of surrender by notable characters, and for these characters, surrender begins with confession.

Gaius Baltar, who becomes an essential religious figurehead by the end of *BSG*, has a moment of confession in the first episode of the season. A woman in his newfound home brings her son to him and asks him to pray that he will live. Gaius didn't expect to be a spiritual leader, and up to this point he was primarily trying to survive execution. Nonetheless, he is drawn to the child and prays a desperate prayer. Laying his hands on the boy's fevered head, he prays,

> Please God, I'm asking you this one last time. Don't let this child die. Has he sinned against you? He can't have sinned against you. He's not even had a life yet. How can you take him and let me live? After all I've done? Really, if you want someone to suffer, take me. We both know I deserve it. I'm selfish and weak. I have failed so many people, and I have killed. I'm not asking for your forgiveness. I'm just asking that you spare the life of this innocent child. Don't take it. Take me. Take, take me. Please.[27]

26. "Daybreak, Part 3," S4, Ep21, directed by Michael Rymer, written by Ronald D. Moore, 0:14:53–0:15:07.

27. "He That Believeth in Me," 0:33:10–0:34:38.

Gaius's confession precedes his surrender to this new life among followers who idolize his teachings.

Laura Roslin also confronts her mortality while receiving cancer treatments. She meets a patient who is closer to death than she is. Emily tells her about visions of the afterlife, confessing her surrender to faith in Gaius Baltar's teachings about God and redemption after death. Laura begins to think about the role of religion in her life, and she also has a vision of crossing a river to a new life where she reunites with departed family.

Later, on the Cylon Baseship, Gaius and Laura are together. Gaius is bleeding to death after an explosion. Laura begins to tend to his wounds. He confesses to her that he feels responsible for the attack on Caprica. He gave the security clearance codes to the Cylons. "I blame myself. I blame myself, but God made the man who made that choice, and God made us all perfect, and in that thought, all my guilt flies away, flies away like a bird."[28] He confesses but also surrenders to the futility. After all, he wasn't aware of what he did.

Baltar's wounds are deep, and he is a bloody mess, lying on a bench with his arms wide, like a crucifix. He lays out a confession of guilt, sin, and the burden that God has lifted by forgiveness. He asks Laura to forgive him as well. She wants to leave him bleeding out, to kill him. She wants justice, but she is confronted at the same time with her own frailty.

As the Baseship makes a series of jumps, Laura meets with her departed spiritual advisor, Elosha. Elosha speaks with her about forgiveness. She confronts Laura with her death and a confession of love from Admiral Adama. After several jumps and many questions, she finally surrenders. She saves Gaius in an act of mercy, and when they return to the *Galactica*, she confesses her love to Adama. Her surrender invigorates her and sets her on a path of healing.

Kara Thrace spends most of the season wondering what she is. Her existential crisis leads her on a journey in which she discovers her own destroyed Viper on Earth, along with the remains of

28. "Hub," 0:30:18–0:30:50.

a corpse wearing military tags identical to her own. Toward the end of the season, she confesses her story to Gaius Baltar. After he publicly reveals she is an angel, she finally surrenders and places her photo on the memorial wall in the *Galactica*. She finds peace within herself, and in the end, she finds the way to Earth.

There are many stories of confession and surrender in the final season of *BSG*. Saul Tigh surrenders to his being a Cylon and reconciles with himself. Adama surrenders *Galactica* to its future as hybrid technology. Ellen Tigh surrenders and agrees to remain with the human fleet. And in the end, on New Earth, the entire fleet surrenders their ships and access to technology to create a new beginning, a second chance for humanity to become better.

CONCLUSION

The final season of *BSG* tells the story of surrender. All the hardships and battle lines that have been drawn since the beginning of the series culminate in the last season of confession, forgiveness, and surrender. Gaius Baltar progresses from a selfish individual to a religious leader and spiritual guru to many people. Laura Roslin takes a spiritual journey where she engages with reason and logic, religious tradition and superstitions, and eventually faith and spirituality, until she is finally at peace with herself, surrendering her own quest for understanding and choosing to live in the solidarity of her community. The Final Five Cylons surrender to full integration with the human fleet and resolve themselves to share in the fate of humanity. In the end, the remnant of humans and Cylons surrender to a new beginning and a fresh start on Earth.

— 5 —

ETHICAL WARNINGS
AND A CHANCE AT
REDEMPTION

FOR A TELEVISION SERIES that set out to provide an interstellar battle with lots of excellent sci-fi-style space battles, *BSG* raised many important questions about personal, spiritual, and moral identity. *BSG* inhabits a space between sci-fi and theology. The series is highly entertaining and can be enjoyed purely for its incredible graphic effects and engaging narrative arc. However, a deeper watch reveals some intense themes that reflect tough ethical questions that, due to the show's insistence on keeping religion at the forefront, are regularly caught up with what God or gods want.

Several issues emerge in ways that may cause discomfort for the viewer. The devastation of losing a large population due to a terrorist attack is, in itself, a heavy subject. The fact that the *BSG Miniseries* was launched only two years after the 9/11 attacks makes this an especially relevant show. While modern fans of *BSG* may not have even been alive at the time of its original launch, the issues raised in the series are still relevant today, and even more so in light of the COVID-19 pandemic.

In the introduction, I explored how science fiction is a genre that purposefully points to ethical issues for humanity. Futurism develops stories in an imagined future that reflects today's human morality. By removing viewers from the realistic present, writers can guide the story to reflect on timeless ethical matters.

In a series such as *BSG* that includes humans as both a created species (by God or the gods) and creators of another species (the Cylons), several layers of ethical considerations are present. Themes explored in the series include the meaning of life, what a creator owes its creation, the significance of difference or sameness in community, family identity, childlessness, divine origination, and genocide, among others. In addition, several religious symbols connect with many of these matters, including sacred space, the existence of angels and other divine beings, prayer, and prophecy.

For this book, I will deal with four themes of identity that contain theological and ethical significance in the series and in the world we inhabit. These include family, children or procreation, interracial relationships or "the Other," and distinction of soul.

FAMILY, A SENSE OF BELONGING

One persistent theme in the series is that of family. With the loss of so much of the human population, it is natural that the definition of family would expand to include friends, close colleagues, and sometimes even rivals. As I referenced earlier, the Cylons and the humans are both seeking to preserve their species. They cannot even imagine cohabitation, but through the first Cylon-human hybrid baby, Hera, they are all saved through shared progeny. Meanwhile, in the desperate state of affairs, regular human family units are inaccessible, and family is formed by proximity and out of necessity.

Laura Roslin, who is promoted to president of the Colonies, lost her family at Caprica. But she is well cared for by her administrative assistant Billy. He knows her and cares for her in a way that stretches the boundaries of professional duty. They become a defacto family unit. They work together for the sake of humanity, but they also hold each other up during this time. The tenderness between the two is apparent from the start. He is quiet, but he notices everything and can anticipate her needs. Laura is alone as president of the Colonies and Billy becomes a close confidant and friend. They are like family.

Laura Roslin and William Adama spend a lot of time in the first season being mistrustful of one another, walking the careful lines that divide military and politics. However, the fighting turns to bickering, and after some time they easily fall into sync with each other to create a military-political hybrid of leadership. They become figureheads that represent parents to the fleet. Adama maintains the stricter, stark lines of militaristic rule, and Laura works in the grey areas to provide for humanity's needs. In many ways, their relationship sets the tone for the family of the fleet. When tensions build up between them, the fleet becomes unstable. As their relationship develops throughout the series, they take on the role of parents, guiding the fleet and holding each other accountable to their respective duties. The series promotes heteronormative family units, including a large-scale family made up of all humans, and, eventually, the allied Cylons.

The crew and their leaders represent the children. Lee Adama is the biological son of William Adama, and ironically he is most at odds with the commander. Starbuck and Col. Tigh, who are not biologically related, are presented to the viewers as enemies from the start, so much at odds with each other that it soon becomes apparent that there are no two people on the *Galactica* that know more about each other than Tigh and Starbuck. They are brother and sister, and both committed absolutely to the leadership of one man—Commander Adama. At the end of the series, Adama tells Starbuck that she is his daughter. Her place is in his family.

William Adama continually presses the *Galactica* crew to think about themselves as a family, eventually extending this notion to include the whole fleet. He stubbornly works to keep the fleet together, recognizing the importance of an inclusive structure. In season two, the fleet threatens to break up, and Adama is the one who acts, referring to the fleet as family. He strives to learn the names of everyone who serves under his command, a habit that becomes very helpful when several Marines join a coup against him to take control of the *Galactica*. He can appeal to each

SO SAY WE ALL

one personally and by name for support. He is like a father figure, uniting all of humanity under his guidance.

Individual family units are also crucial in *BSG*. On New Caprica, the survivors form nuclear family units: children and parents live together in small barracks. Almost immediately upon arriving on the planet, people break into smaller family groups focused on male/female couplings. Kara Thrace and Sam Anders get married, followed by Lee Adama and Lt. Dualla. Admiral Adama and Laura Roslin dream about a future together where they build a cabin by the lake. Tigh and Ellen renew their commitment to their partnership as well. Tyrol and Cally marry and care for a baby together. On the *Galactica*, Helo and Sharon together grieve the supposed loss of their baby. In the Cylon quarters, Leoben finally makes progress connecting with Kara Thrace when he brings her a "daughter," so they form a small, independent family.

The virtue of family in *BSG* centers on the family unit as a mother, a father, and children. This is exemplified on a large scale with the ship and its crew, and in smaller individual family units. This model of family aligns with the moral and ethical values of modern Abrahamic faith religions—one man, one woman, and children, or at least the hope for children.

The only exception to the family unit among humans is where Laura helps raise the Cylon-human hybrid child, Hera, with another woman in secret. Of course, since Hera is an exceptional child and character in the series, it is not unusual to be raised in an exceptional context. Hera is cared for in various contexts before she is finally raised by her biological parents on Earth.

The Cylons also organize in a familial way. They sustain a community of equity by encouraging input from every Cylon. Particular models value the family structure. For example, the Cavil model call each other "brother," and the Eights refer to each other as "sister." The Cylons are united in purpose initially, but as the series proceeds, they divide based on individual values of faith.

The larger picture of family extends beyond the ships or the fleet—humanity is parent to the Cylon. Humans are parent-creators. The Cylons refer to themselves as children of humans, stating that parents must die so that the children can fulfill their potential. Meanwhile, the humans call the Cylons their creation, stating their right to destroy them.

PROGENY AND PROCREATION

Anxiety about the ability to procreate is pervasive in sci-fi stories. Many books, films, and series explore a future where procreation might not be possible. *BSG* is no exception. A family that provides for human companionship and intimacy is vital in the series, but a family that provides for the next generation is essential. Emphasis on the family is a well-attested religious theme. Nearly all of the world's religions value having children and see it as a divine blessing. In a science-fictional future, human rights and technology are sometimes at odds with the miraculous, like the creation of life by organic means. However, in *BSG*, there are two forms of procreation. The humans created the Cylons, who have become sentient beings, and they also procreate by having children. Furthermore, the birth of the child Hera demonstrates that procreation between humans and Cylons is also possible. Hera's existence proves the possibility of a future where humans and Cylons live peacefully together.

Procreation is a theme visited from both human and Cylon perspectives in *BSG*. Humans not only need to preserve the lives they have, but they must consider increasing the human population before they become extinct. The Cylons want to have babies to become a self-sufficient and diverse population, viewed as a blessing from God. Humans want to have babies so they can repopulate and save their species. The series also calls attention to the death of children and genocide in general.

The *BSG Miniseries* introduced the genocidal plan of the Cylons to wipe out all human life, and it starts when Caprica Six breaks the neck of a tiny infant, feeling no remorse as she does so. If there is any innocence to be had, it is her expressed curiosity about the fragility of human life. She is justified by recognizing she will save the baby from a much more painful death. Six's action is the precursor to the Cylons' desired outcome: the genocide of the entire human race.

As the initial story line progresses, we get another indicator of humanity's impending doom when a young girl is the focus of the newly inducted President Roslin's visit to a civilian ship in the Colonial Fleet. When the tough decision is made hours later to leave a compromised ship behind, Billy reminds the president (and the viewer) that the little girl she met was destroyed in that action, not to mention the hundreds of other humans aboard. The image of one small child reminds us of the vulnerability of an entire human population.

The murder of a child is a theme familiar to religious stories. In the Hebrew Bible, Abraham threatens to sacrifice his child, Isaac, in Genesis. In Exodus, Pharaoh orders the killing of all Hebrew baby boys at the time Moses is born. In the Christian New Testament is Herod's order to kill all baby boys around the time of Jesus' birth. Each of these stories contains a subversive element, people fighting against a common enemy to save a vulnerable population, and in each of these stories a salvific figure is spared. In the sacrifice of Isaac, it is a ram of God's provision; in response to Pharaoh's order, Moses led the Hebrew slaves out of Egypt; and under Herod, it was the birth of Jesus Christ that brought deliverance.

The Cylon's willingness to kill a small child and her advocacy of genocide places the Cylons neatly among other religious villains. But the theme accomplishes something else—it heralds the coming of a savior. Each of these stories anticipates a messiah.

A specific child is prophesied about in season two. The baby is carried by a Cylon mother, Sharon, and fathered by a human, Helo. When Sharon finds out she is pregnant, she explains that one of God's commandments is to be fruitful. These words are reminiscent of the command in Genesis 1:28 to "be fruitful and multiply." Head Six takes the opportunity to teach Gaius Baltar about the importance of children and God's design for procreation. She convinces him that he will be a "father" and protector of the child, inheriting by adoption. It is his spiritual role according to God's plan.

In a vision, Gaius hands the baby Hera to Adama, and he places the baby in the river and walks away, leaving the child to drown. In season one, a Cylon murders a baby. In the next season, humanity's leader killed a baby that represented reconciliation between humans and Cylon. These babies are ciphers for the vulnerability of each race.

Both the Cavil and the Six models talk about themselves as children of humanity. Cavil displays a kind of childlike jealousy of humankind. He was the first one created in humanity's image, and he resents it. Six has a different approach. She believes Cylons have outgrown their human parents, and at one point suggests that children can never really be free to live their fullest potential until they kill their parents.

Like in the previous two seasons, season three gives us a small child in the opening scenes. Kacy is a toddler that Leoben presents to Starbuck as "her child," born from artificial reproductive technologies. Starbuck does not want to engage with the child, and she distances herself until Kacy falls down the stairway and is seriously injured. She has hit her head and is bleeding. Unlike in previous episodes, this baby does not die. Again the viewer is confronted with the importance of children and attention to the next generation. The child-centered family is prioritized as a model of responsible procreation.

The ethic of the child-centered family is often tied to religious ideologies. Still, childbearing as an economic factor becomes a priority when the survival of an entire species is at risk. Laura Roslin is a political liberal, and as such, she makes the preservation of human souls a significant priority, but this means supporting procreation over abortion rights. In the very first episode, the *BSG Miniseries*, she tells Adama that people need to hurry up and make babies if they are going to survive the attempted genocide of the human race.

Among those in the fleet, small child-centered family units have sprung up everywhere. Cally and Chief are raising a baby and need childcare while they work. There is also a refugee camp with families aboard. After Helo and Sharon discover Hera is still alive, they rescue her. When Sharon picks up her baby, there is a recognizable bond. Boomer notices Hera's response to Sharon. She comments aloud that Hera recognizes her mother, even though all the eights are identical. Boomer threatens Hera's life and Caprica Six snaps Boomer's neck before helping Sharon escape. Caprica Six snapped a human baby's neck in the *BSG Miniseries*, and her deference to protecting Hera is significant. Hera is not just any baby. She is a human-Cylon hybrid, the "shape of things to come." After the crew return from New Caprica, children and family become even more central to the life of *Galactica*.

Once the Final Five Cylons are revealed, we find they are parents to the other Cylon models. The humans created them, they evolved, and then created the other Cylon models. Their decision to remain with the human fleet at the end of the series is an act of familial reconciliation and an attempt to break the cycle that children are born to replace their parents.

At the end of the series, the child Hera, who was born as a Cylon-human hybrid, becomes the first in a lineage of people that inhabit the newly settled planet at the end of the series. Salvation is procured through the propagation of the species. In the end, unity is procured through peaceful cohabitation and a shared genetic profile through organic procreation.

DISENFRANCHISING THE "OTHER"

Disenfranchisement is an ongoing theme in *BSG*. More specifically, "Who is the *Other*?" This question accesses the other side of "family." Instead of identifying who belongs, it seeks to disenfranchise those who are other for the sake of homogenous security. In season one, the boundaries of the *Other* are secure. Humans on one side and Cylon on the other. The Cylon seeks the genocide of humanity, leaving humans vulnerable. Even though the humans would like nothing less than to eviscerate the Cylons, they have been weakened nearly to extinction and now must do everything to preserve their species.

The menacing threat of genocide preempts the vulnerability of the human population, a theme visited throughout the *BSG* series from both human and Cylon perspectives. When backed into a corner, human agents resort to suicide bombings to take out the Cylons—both humans and Cylons work to destroy the other. The concept of killing a species for its bad behavior is also explored in the Hebrew Bible. Consider the flood narrative, beginning in Genesis 6, which effectively describes the destruction of nearly all of the human race. In the record, the Creator God reserves the right to destroy all that was created. In the case of humans, they might claim this justification too. They made the Cylons, and the power of destruction might well be in their hands. For the Cylons, they are attempting to destroy their human creators.

Religious stories of mass destruction and the clearing of huge populations often accompany the recognition of an eternal quality of life, an enduring soul. Religious stories of mass destruction emphasize the enduring soul. Sometimes this takes the form of an ineffable quality of individual existence, a personal soul that outlives the body. Other times, eternal life happens by means of procreation; the genetic material lives on in the next generation. Procreation is seen as a blessing to protect a species from mass extinction. The religious themes in *BSG* herald certain ideologies taught in catechism or Sunday school: genocide is primarily motivated by the pursuit of holy or divine attention and subsequent blessing. Whether human or Cylon, both justified their violent actions by insisting on pure motives and a right to live.

Defining the *Other* against the family leads to a question about who belongs in the *Galactica* family, and by extension the human fleet. When Commander Adama awakens after Boomer shoots him, he faces a philosophical crisis. How could Boomer be like family when she was a Cylon all along? He questions whether one can love a machine. Tyrol loved her, and because of that love, she was more than a machine. By the end of the series, Adama fully accepts the likeness between Cylons and humans. But, Tyrol, who we discover is a Cylon, has gone the other way. He tells Helo that his love is an illusion because machines cannot love the same way a human can. Tyrol argues for distinct categories, especially in matters of the heart, but his words come too late in the series to take effect. In the end, the audience accepts Cylons as part of the human remnant.

The series constantly presses the question of who belongs with us versus who belongs to our enemies. In season two, the *Pegasus* shows up, and we get a glimpse of the dark side of martial law. Compromise can be a good thing for the sake of humanity's integrity. Adama faces the question he posed in his very first speech—Is humanity even worth saving?

At the very beginning of the series, the designations are simple. The "us" is the human fleet, and the "other" is the Cylon. By the time we get to season three, the designation is less clear. *Other* identities depend on the individual distinction. Among the humans, refugees and other lower-status humans are *Othered* by discrimination over religious and political differences. This is not an exclusively human trait. Even factions develop between the Cylons as tensions grow between the models.

In season three, a clear and relevant example of religious discrimination in the human fleet can be found in the episode "The Woman King." The Sagittarons are a colony that segregates themselves from the masses based on religious principles. The doctor in service to the refugee civilians is prejudiced against them, confiding in Saul Tigh that "aside from a Cylon, is there anything you hate more than a Sagittaron?"[1] With the Cylon threat at bay, humans go back to doing what they do best by creating factions, dividing themselves via social interests. Another episode, "Dirty Hands," explores inherent and systemic violence in the default model where children inherit jobs from their parents. Due to the confined nature of starship travel, inheriting jobs was accepted as a pragmatic solution, even though it posed a clear violation of free and democratic social standards. To the credit of the *BSG*, these issues were addressed with careful equanimity. *Galactica*'s leaders

1. "The Woman King," S3, Ep14, directed by Michael Rymer, written by Michael Taylor, 0:40:26–0:40:32.

proved to be patient listeners and gracious with understanding, a model we could use as examples for our natural world leaders.

Over the four seasons, the clarity of "Us-versus-Them" dissipates, and enemies are potentially anywhere. This reality climaxes when the Final Five Cylons are revealed to be members of the human fleet all along. All of a sudden, there is a shift in perception. Tyrol, Tigh, Ellen, Anders, and Tory were completely human up until the final season. The revelation of these five—and their subsequent shared existential crises—completely shifts the viewer's vantage point. How can we continue to fight a war when our own kind, our own family, are among the enemy? The lines become blurred to the point that we are unable to distinguish between us and them.

In the series, Gaius Baltar makes the most apparent progress in seeing from the perspective of the *Other.* At first, he is in alignment with their purpose, even to destroy the humans via mass genocide, but his shifting perspective is a religious conversion, not political realignment. His change comes from religious enlightenment and faith in God. As Baltar opens his heart to accept the love of a perfect God, he can also accept the Cylons on equal terms. In many ways, his faults and cowardice aside, Gaius Baltar is the voice of unity and inclusion for the disenfranchised members of the fleet.

The one thing that seems to bring equality for humans and Cylons is the destruction of the Resurrection Ship and its technology. The Cylons who ally with the humans argue that mortality is what makes life worth living. Once everyone has one life to live, they are equal. However, it is not until the *Galactica* becomes a complete blend of humans and Cylon technology that the boundaries of "us" and "them" genuinely dissipate. When several human and Cylon repair technicians die together in a ship malfunction, they are all united in a way through funerary services for their lost loved ones. *Galactica* becomes a blended ship, representing the marriage of two communities—human and Cylon.

DISTINCTION OF SOUL

The value of life as a whole and individual souls is a theme that emerges right away in *BSG*. With the destruction of the colony planets and the subsequent destruction of several space vessels, the remaining human survivors make up humanity's last chance to survive as a species. Season one focuses on the depletion of the human race as Laura tracks the population numbers on a whiteboard above her desk. She counts them as souls in recognition of the unique and ethereal status of each human being. The population figure is a sign of hope that humanity has not yet become extinct, but it also recognizes the near genocide by the Cylon attack. Each living human being matters, even if for no other reason than with so many lost, the regrowth of the human population will be a slow journey, even if they manage to resettle in another world.

The implication of every person having a soul, an essence of life that makes them unique, is reflected in the state of the Cylon as well. The Cylon does not die in the same way as a human. However, the sum of their memories are uploaded to a new body, and what are we, but the sum of our memories? Later in the series, when Cylon models begin to differentiate from the others of their kind, they do so because of their experience of interacting intimately with humans.

Caprica Six and Boomer are Cylons, but they are distinct from other Sixes and Eights because they have become sympathetic to humanity. They have both lived among humans. They each experience romantic love that served to override their programming. The experience of love changed them. This is a recurrent theme in *BSG*. Whether attributed to the fulfillment of divine purpose or self-gratification, the Cylons who experience love also experience change. This is also true of the bond between child and mother. Hera recognizes her mother as distinct from other identical Model Eight Cylons. This seems to indicate the existence of particular and individual identity even among identical Cylon models. Is this evidence of a soul?

Personhood, or the distinction between body and mind, is highlighted as well. There is a strong theme of physicality in descriptions of blood and body. When Boomer is shot at the beginning of season two, her blood drips to the metal floor of the *Galactica*. The building of the Blackbird shows hope for a new body, a new class of ship. Laura's progressing cancer diminishes her body while her mind and spirit remain strong. Sharon grows life inside her organically, like a human woman. Gaius points out that the Cylon blood is indistinguishable from human blood, and the hybrid child's blood cures Laura's cancer. Sharon rips open her skin, plugs into the *Galactica* like a machine, and saves the ship. At the same time, she renders the Cylon Raiders vulnerable to attack, and they are massacred in blood and guts. On Kobol, Laura refers to the cost in blood when her priest dies in an explosion. She recovers the torn and damaged Book of Pythia, the blood-soaked survivor. Cylon and humans share a common experience of bodily interaction with the world.

On the other hand, we are exposed to shared emotional, mental trauma experienced by Cylons and humans. Gina, who is violently raped and tortured aboard the *Pegasus,* prefers death without resurrection to the traumatic torment of memory of her experience. Sharon becomes lost in her grief after her baby is declared dead. Tyrol experiences violent outbursts and waking nightmares. On the Baseship that became infected with a Cylon-specific virus, Cylons gather to hold hands and say a prayer, recognizing their final death without hope for resurrection. They are self-aware and grieve the loss of the individual in the act of religious contrition.

When the Cylons have resurrection capabilities, they are like reincarnated beings, their consciousness and experiences uploaded to a new body to compile experiences. Just before the Resurrection Hub is destroyed, Helo and Sharon unbox the D'Anna model, and they get a view of all the "unborn" or "unused" Cylon bodies. Copies upon copies upon copies lie dormant in liquid baths, each one waiting for a consciousness. Mass quantity decreases the value of the body. Substance is found in the limited space of mortality.

While there are some attempts to draw connections between the Cylon's resurrection and Buddhism, there are significant differences. For one thing, the memories of all previously lived experiences remain intact. Also, the body remains the same model, meaning the embodied experience is the same. Perhaps it is for this reason that Cavil continually repeats the idea that the Cylons are machines that rely on technology for resurrection, and the concept of a soul is irrelevant. Without mortality, any potential soul is trapped in the eternal loop of a singular existence.

The soul's rebirth in the afterlife when a person's body dies is a major theme in the last season. Laura experiences a vision of the crossing of a river after death when Emily, another cancer patient, dies. Later, when a Six Cylon dies in the medical ward, she describes a similar vision—trees, a river. Regardless of race, the soul is distinct from the body and may live on after the body dies. Viewers get a glimpse of an afterlife that is vague and distant. After the Cylon Resurrection Ship is destroyed, the spiritual significance of an eternal soul in a physical and temporal body is shared by both Cylon and human.

ALL THIS HAS HAPPENED BEFORE

The question raised by events at the end of the series is, "Must this all happen again?" The humans and Cylons deliberately work to break the cycles of destruction that have wrapped up their past. One of the ways they do this is by denying the old gods. The gods, named for the familiar Greco-Roman deities (i.e., Zeus, Athena, Apollo), perpetuate cycles of war and pride. The faith that *BSG* introduces in response is one of reconciliation, hope, and surrender.

There are many questions left unanswered in the series, one of which is the future of AI on New Earth. The implicit suggestion is that the same old patterns have emerged. Humans create robots to serve their needs. As an ethical practice, it does not matter if they are sentient. Humans will have to decide whether (and how) to practice a measure of moral restraint in their treatment of machines, whether they are seen as equals or not. *BSG* has offered a warning. *Othering* leads to more significant trouble. There is a better path.

The fleet's choice to sacrifice their technology and the potential to rebuild Caprica on Earth offers an opportunity to hope for a better cycle this time, ending cyclical failure. Yet, humans seem doomed to become the creators of their own demise. This is no insignificant warning for the viewer. The characters in the story have lived out the worst and the best of what humanity offers. Now, it is for the audience to decide whether we will choose redemption for ourselves. We have an opportunity to identify the good and choose for ourselves before it all happens again.

— 6 —

CONCLUSION

THE BIG REVEAL AT the end of the *BSG* series is the implicit suggestion that the Cylon-human fleet landed on our Earth when humans were still living in tribes. Finally, we get the payoff for the phrase "All this has happened before, and it will all happen again." Our future hangs in the balance of our hubris. *BSG* is undoubtedly famous for its amazing graphic effects and entertaining quality, but the series takes a profound philosophical approach to matters of human faith and acceptance. By placing humans like us in a distant galaxy and a unique technological future, the audience is forced to wrestle with questions of morality and ethics that are indeed related to the world we inhabit, without the stakes of commenting on real-world scenarios.

As much as *BSG* was about humanity's interaction with technology and the will to survive, the show was heavily invested in exploring the influence of religious ideals. Furthermore, the series itself took religion seriously and believed the religious ideas it posed. The fact that so many viewers have identified with various elements in the series and younger viewers continue to connect nearly two decades after its introduction says something about the connection of faith and people. *BSG* touched on something important in drawing out a desire to understand ourselves and our existence by learning what it is to be mortal, what it means to be part of a family, to have children, to reach out to those who are marginalized, and to recognize the eternal existence of the soul.

Religion in *Battlestar Galactica* is not the fullness of the story, but it shines where humans insist on faith, and that happens for everyone, everywhere. Even the agnostic Cylon "priest" Cavil has to reconcile a discussion about the merits of belief in a soul, which he considers an exclusively human matter. But this turns out not to be the case. His arrogance causes disillusion. When the Cylons relinquish access to the Resurrection Hub, they gain access to the human afterlife across the river. Ironically, it is the agnostic human scientist who is most fully converted and religion's most active advocate in *BSG*. Gaius Baltar learns how to have faith, and then instructs others in it. His journey is complete in the end when he fully surrenders to becoming a farmer on New Earth, his inheritance, the role he had been running from all his life.

A famous photo of the *BSG* characters reenacts the fifteenth-century Leonardo Da Vinci mural painting, *Il Cenacolo, The Last Supper*. The picture portrays Head Six, the Six Cylon/angel who haunts Gaius Baltar, in the center, in the position of Christ. Immediately to her left is Gaius Baltar, who dons green and blue, the same colors as Judas, the Betrayer, who sits to the left of Christ. The others may not have clear connections to the twelve apostles Da Vinci painted. Still, it is of note that Laura Roslin and Bill Adama sit on either side of the table, anchoring the group as they turn slightly toward each other. Chief Tyrol is angrily holding a knife, perhaps portraying a version of Thomas, who raises a finger in anger and also sits on the right side of Christ in Da Vinci's version. Furthermore, there is one missing, who should sit to the right of Saul Tigh, behind the green chalice. This might hold a place for Ellen, who died drinking poison on New Caprica and was resurrected. This photo was a promotional marketing image used for publicity. The religious themes in *BSG* are explicit to its story, connecting the series to Western faith traditions.

My purpose in drawing out the religious themes in this series was to identify the interconnectedness of religion and sci-fi. Many sci-fi stories develop explicit religious themes or implicitly draw on existing religious paradigms. But what makes *BSG* such a great case study is that it not only creates multiple religious factions and draws upon real-world human faith traditions, but the show itself also believes in the religion. It is not merely an illusion that angels exist; they *do* exist. The afterlife is not a limited and arbitrary experience; it is universal and freely offered. Sacrifice comes with a reward, and unity is the goal of love. If there ever was a television series that confronts humanity's desire to uphold an agnostic virtue of science in favor of a universal faith that leads to reconciliation and peace, it is *Battlestar Galactica*.

So say we all.